Wedding Planning

Plan the Perfect Wedding and Avoid Potential Mistakes

(How to Plan Your Dream Wedding, That's Beautiful, Elegant and Royal)

Megan Callahan

Published By **Jackson Denver**

Megan Callahan

Wedding Planning: Plan the Perfect Wedding and Avoid Potential Mistakes (How to Plan Your Dream Wedding, That's Beautiful, Elegant and Royal)

ISBN   978-1-998901-46-3

No part of this guidebook shall be reproduced in any form without permission in writing from the publisher except in the case of brief quotations embodied in critical articles or reviews.

Legal & Disclaimer

The information contained in this ebook is not designed to replace or take the place of any form of medicine or professional medical advice. The information in this ebook has been provided for educational & entertainment purposes only.

The information contained in this book has been compiled from sources deemed reliable, and it is accurate to the best of the Author's knowledge; however, the Author cannot guarantee its accuracy and validity and cannot be held liable for any errors or omissions. Changes are periodically made to this book. You must consult your doctor or get professional medical advice before using any of the suggested remedies, techniques, or information in this book.

Upon using the information contained in this book, you agree to hold harmless the Author from and against any damages, costs, and expenses, including any legal fees potentially resulting from the application of any of the information provided by this guide. This disclaimer applies to any damages or injury caused by the use and application, whether directly or indirectly, of any advice or information presented, whether for breach of contract, tort, negligence, personal injury, criminal intent, or under any other cause of action.

You agree to accept all risks of using the information presented inside this book. You need to consult a professional medical practitioner in order to ensure you are both able and healthy enough to participate in this program.

Table Of Contents

Chapter 1: Choosing Your Wedding Party

In the beginning in this publication, I recommended you and your partner meet together when discussing all the aspects in your wedding. The size of your wedding celebration isn't an exception.

The traditional wedding reception was comprised of a mix of family and friends , including women from the side of the bride and men on the groom's side.

The current trend has expanded to include a wide variety of configurations. It's not uncommon to see a woman who is the best as a substitute for the top man, or weddings with diverse number of guests.

Some couples choose to leave out the tradition altogether due to diverse reasons. This could be due to budgetary constraints or having numerous family members and friends who they don't wish to offend or simply want all the attention to be placed solely on themselves.

Consider the people you would like to be with. Then, try to select your wedding celebration based the true desires and feelings about these people.

If you've been to 30 weddings, do not think that you must have 30 bridesmaids for the wedding to make your wedding "fair". A wedding which is too large can cause more stress and stress during the process of planning a wedding.

Consider the personality of your close friends and ask yourself if they all be friends? Are they the kind of people I imagine when I think of my wedding day? Or are they people who tend to cause unneeded drama?

A good amount is not more than five persons on either side, and three being the perfect number.

You should be considerate of couples. Do they have been together for all the time? Are you familiar with them both well? If yes, then include them each. This will make the process simpler for them as well as you in the end.

Tuxedo Rentals

There's a reason I didn't give information on the groom's outfit in the first chapter, and that's because If you are having a wedding celebration, the groom's suit should be tied with the tuxes of the groomsmen.

I worked for a tuxedo business and found that many have promotions that are beneficial to the groom.

In the case of a wedding If all the groomsmen's ushers, groomsmen and fathers purchase their tuxes from the same store, the groom is likely to get the rental at no cost. This is a fantastic method of reducing the cost and there is a good chance that you or your spouse were in an event before, you've helped a friend with a tux rental by renting theirs to them for the wedding.

If you opt to do this take note to the cost of groomsmen's weddings. They have a goal of selling you more and the best method of doing that is to constantly remind the groom that they will not be charged for any of the extras you select.

Be cautious as some of these charges might not appear to be due to the way the salesperson explains it. It could be something like "So you'll need the socks, pocket square and cuff-links as well" while the salesperson is checking the boxes on the system. This will add an additional $15 to $30 per tuxedo without even having any idea.

It's okay if you were thinking of including them and the cost was what you anticipated, however, if it wasn't you should know about this practice and inquire upfront about the total cost before adding them to your order.

Consider the weather conditions on the day of your wedding. Most tuxedos are chosen months in advance , allowing the measurement and ordering. It is tempting to choose warm, wool tuxes as you braved the winter storm to get to the boutique and only to have those who are groomsmen sweating buckets of sweat during the July wedding outside.

Beware of big name brands. In comparison with dresses, formal tuxedos offer very little difference between them.

Utilize this advantage to your advantage. If you're looking for a reasonable priced tuxedo, and the salesperson is trying to convince you to buy the same model with a brand name which is $75 more expensive because , in their mind "you don't have to pay to buy it".

Keep sticking keep the one you loved initially. I guarantee your groomsmen will be grateful for it.

Alternative Options

Consider your idea of a theme. Simply because they're popular it doesn't mean you have to buy wedding tuxedos for your groomsmen.

If you're planning an informal, simple wedding on the beach, a black 3-piece suit with tails looks quite odd. Tan linen pants and white dress shirts that have no ties will look better and will be more comfortable for the groomsmen. Also, they will save money.

Bridesmaids

I'm going to begin this article with a public service message for all women who have ever served as bridesmaids.

Your Bridesmaids Do NOT Have to Match Exactly.

Yes, they do. This is unless you believe in the belief system that began the "they must be in line with" tradition.

The time of Roman time, Romans believed that evil spirits would show up at weddings as a way to curse the bride and groom.

The method they used to combat this was to make the minimum of 10 guests wear clothes that were similar to what the groom and bride were wearing for the purpose to confuse the spirits and bringing luck to the wedding.

Therefore, unless you believe in this myth and you plan to invite 10 guests to your wedding, wearing wedding dresses. It is possible to dispel this myth.

Pick a Color

It is likely that you have bridesmaids who have different styles, preferences and kinds. You'll be adored by them if instead of having every bridesmaid wear the size 2 strapless dress, you allow them to have a little flexibility. Also, they won't be forced to wander around the wedding throughout the night, chasing bizarre twins of themselves.

A trend that is growing and welcomed is to select the color of the dress that you want all bridesmaids in and giving them the option of choosing the type of dress they will wear according to their individual desires, preferences, and body kind.

This is a fantastic idea since, first and most importantly, they get to select a dress they'll wear for the rest of their lives.

This is an enormous benefit. When you spend lots of money on an item of clothing, it's nice to wear it more than one time. As with many other women, I own a dress that cost me two hundred dollars stored in my closet, which I'll never wear again. Don't make the same mistake to your loved ones.

They can also find an affordable dress.

To go into more detail on this issue, peer pressure is a powerful force. Peer pressure when shopping with brides and other women you have not known, is more powerful.

The $300 dress could be "just right" for a few of your bridesmaids, but for those who didn't want to appear as "difficult or costly" it might require a lot of sacrifices for months to have the money to participating in your wedding.

It's simple to become caught in the chaos of emotions during the planning of your wedding, and sometimes it's even easy to forget that your wedding is not as important to other people like it's to you. Your family and friends are busy and full of stress-inducing moments Don't let your wedding be one of them.

Contrary to what the popular wedding show might claim that your bridesmaids should to feel it's an honor to be participant in your wedding and not an unlucky fate. They were chosen because of your are devoted to your bridesmaids, so make sure you give them the same love and respect. A budget-breaking decision is not an option.

This includes makeup, hair spa treatments as well as shoes, jewelry, and everything else that is required to make bridesmaids. This is not even including bridal showers, bachelorette events. These expenses do add up fast.

Make yourself the most perfect bride by always offering choices, while making sure that you are keeping your bridesmaids' comfort at your mind at all times.

Wedding Party Gifts

The rehearsal dinner is where some brides and grooms opt to present their wedding guests with presents as a small gesture of their gratitude.

This could include anything from hand-crafted jewelry for weddings to whiskey bottles to personalized flasks and watches. You can be really individual and unique without having to shell out an enormous amount of cash.

Do your wedding guests have a few things in common? Are they book enthusiasts? Gamers? Hikers? Hipsters? Coffee-lovers? Fine alcohol drinkers?

I'm sure you're getting the picture It's likely that you have interests or hobbies that you share because you're all close friends. Utilize these interests to narrow down the kind of gifts you'd like to buy.

My husband and his buddies have a passion for pocket watches. Mom and I managed to negotiate a very good deal with a local watch shop to get personalized pocket watches for the guys in the wedding celebration.

We got a lower price since we purchased them all in one go and they didn't all fit. The difference in the fact that they did not coincided was just what we needed since we wanted them all to be different, but of course I didn't tell the salesperson selling the watches know this (Negotiating 101).

Going the Extra Mile

There's no need to limit yourself to wedding gifts. The guests at your wedding are going to spend the entire wedding day chasing around you and your partner. Doing errands and getting ready and making sure aunt Mildred far from the bars.

Why not create some sort of survival kit for each one? It doesn't need to cost an enormous amount, but it will make a difference to your loved ones.

I went to the dollar store and came across many small things that could make their lives more enjoyable.

Here's an example:

Flip-flops (for worn-out feet)

Tissues

Travel stain remover

Hairspray

Mints

Medicine for headaches

Chapstick

Combs

Bobby Pins

The sky is can be the limit. Make this a reality using the canvas bags from dollar stores and you'll have everything you need to have everything you need for that wedding.

Chapter 2: How To Save On Wedding Decorations

Decorate! It's a great aspect of the process, but is a simple process that can go from budget-friendly to expensive, particularly when you've got a huge imagination. If you have a big imagination but we'll utilize it to get imaginative to create stunning and affordable decors.

Flowers

Perhaps the most costly item for decorating budgets, with an average cost of between $60 and $80 for a floral centerpiece, it's not surprising that the average cost of flowers across America increases to more than $2000.

Okay, now don't stress out. Relax. There are methods to save a significant amount of money for flowers , while still getting the appearance you desire.

DIY

My wedding was a dream for me. I wanted pink roses as centerpieces. It could easily been 10 times what we actually spent for an online florist to create our centerpieces.

We chose to go instead the DIY way. You might be asking whether you grew yourself flowers? It's not even very close. My husband says there is a problem with my black thumb, and he has reasons. There's no reason to get things complicated by having to plant and pick the flowers you want.

We live in a fantastic age of the internet. Never before did brides have access to information and numerous options to pick from. From the past to weddings, you can have everything in your hands and wedding flowers aren't an the exception.

Do you know it is possible to place an order for flowers on the internet? Wholesale costs? and that you could buy DIY kits that include every single flower that you will need to create your own centerpieces that are designed by you as well as boutonnieres, corsages and much more? Yes, these businesses are incredible and great for brides who are who is on a tight budget.

Fiftyflowers.com

I made use of fiftyflowers.com to plan my wedding, and could not be more satisfied. I purchased the roses package and just wanted to point out that 200 roses can take up a lot of space. Be prepared to have an icy dark room with plenty of water buckets for the flowers.

If you're not a DIY person, fiftyflowers.com also has premade centerpieces, boutonnieres, and corsages for sale. They also offer a custom design package dubbed "Wedding Flowers in A Box" that allows them to create, coordinate and arrange all the floral arrangements for you all in one box.

Costco

Are you a Costco member? If yes, you are able to purchase bulk bouquets of flowers from Costco too. They are currently offering 12 bouquets of roses (144 branches) for just $119.99. It is worth looking into.

Farmers Market

Another option to DIY is one of my friends used with success. There's a great farmers market in our town that has a wide variety of flowers. The reception was an outdoors, casual wedding, so she was not picky about the kind of flowers she preferred. She simply wanted a simple, stunning and simple appearance.

Her parents were enlisted on for the day before their wedding (this was scheduled weeks ahead) to attend the farmers market from the moment it began to open. Her parents had an idea of the she wanted to wear and the colors and they arranged it on the stands for flowers.

Since they arrived early and planning to purchase a large number of flowers, they were able to get the most beautiful assortment of flowers, but they were also able to secure the best price for them.

What if I don't do my own DIY?

If you're not interested in making your own flowers there are many options to reduce the cost of arrangements for flowers. Apart from the wholesale option mentioned above, there's a second location where you can get together with a florist one-on one. You can also get custom-arranged flowers that offer excellent customer service. This isn't the only specialty florist shop.

What's this site? A local grocery store. Yes. That's right. The local supermarkets have professional florists who offer amazing costs. Because we planned to put together all of the centerpieces by ourselves, I was unsure of how to create boutonnieres, bouquets, corsages or floral headbands. We decided to ask for the assistance from our local supermarket. We went to the new Hyvee store in our area however almost all grocery stores across the United States has a floral department.

The floral designer sat down with us for an hour , flipping through books full of gorgeous arrangements. She was on time and was able to work within the budget we had set. On the day of our wedding, the flowers were stunning than we had hoped for.

Decorating

After choosing your wedding venue and figuring out the number of guests you're likely to invite. You'll be better equipped to determine what you'll require to decorate your wedding.

Take a look at what this venue can offer. It is likely that they have provided all napkins, tablecloths, tables and chairs.

Some even provide centerpieces and other decorating services at no cost. Others will offer these services, but at the cost of a large amount. If your venue is offering these services at free then take advantage of the deal. This can make you save a significant amount of dollars in the long run.

The theme you spouse and you have decided on, now you can narrow your focus to those elements that you would like to tie everything together.

For instance, if you are looking for a casual and rustic look with a burlap runner or white candles with mason jars with wildflowers are an easy and elegant style that can express the theme.

If you've been thinking of a wedding in the past, bring your vision for your guest by covering the tables with different tablecloths from the past and top them off with small antique cake pedestals or vase with vintage wedding cake "bride and groom" toppers.

Perhaps you and your fiancé like books and a tabletop of your old-fashioned books beautifully stacked is the only way to show your personality.

Isn't it exciting? The choice of a theme will allow you to define the limits that your imagination can fly with imaginative ideas to make your wedding unique.

Craft Stores

Subscribe to Michael's or Joann Fabrics' email coupons. Make sure to only purchase from these stores when you have coupons. They have plenty of them each weekend, either online or in the local paper. One of the most well-known offering a 40% discount on one thing. It's a lot when it comes to buying items for a wedding.

Every occasionally, they'll release 20% off the entire purchase of sale, regular and clearance priced products coupon. This coupon will result in significant discounts for the customer. Check out the shops for the items you'll require, and then use coupons wisely in the planning of your wedding.

Internet

Before you leave, please else , use the internet.

Look up amazon.com, etsy.com, orientaltrading.com, shindigz.com, and other well-known party websites. Doing a search before purchasing online could mean the difference between spending excessively and making a huge savings.

If you spot some thing you want in the particular store and you like it, then search for it. Check if the price is affordable. Do you have a better price? Make sure you include handling and shipping when comparing prices. There might be a lower price on the internet, but should all of your savings are wiped out due to the high cost of shipping, purchase the item from the shop instead.

Prior to purchasing on the internet, you must search the name of the site and also the word "coupon code" on your preferred search engine. If you do this on your own you will be able to find coupons that can reduce shipping costs or even a portion of the total amount of the purchase.

Also, you can read the reviews on the websites. Are they rated as a good site by users? Do they have lots or negative comments? Do they have a large number of negative reviews? There are plenty of reputable sites online to avoid purchasing from sites that are that are less than trustworthy.

You can think outside of the wedding, event or craft shop

Locations such as Marshalls, TJ Maxx, Big Lots and even Goodwill are the best places to search for those cheap accessories that can improve your decor.

My wedding was themed around travel with vintage luggage that we bought at Goodwill for $5 helped to complete the décor without costing a lot within my financial budget.

Favors

Do you actually need gifts? It's possible you won't buy them , and that's completely fine. However, if you decide to. Find something your guests actually will benefit from.

A sculpture of you and your your fiancee is lovely. I doubt that many people who attend your wedding will find a spot or desire to display the statues in their home.

Food-based or useful favors are an excellent idea. If you're planning an autumn wedding and you are planning to have a caramel apple, then apple caramel wrapped with cellophane are the perfect present. Delicious sugar cookies decorated to match the theme is a low-cost and sure to please.

Elegant wine stoppers or bottle openers make great presents that your guests will appreciate and cherish for many years to be.

Anything that's inexpensive tasty, practical or useful and reflects your personal style can be the perfect gift of your bridal guests.

I believe this is among the most enjoyable aspects of organizing the wedding. You can be imaginative and come up with unique ways to express your creative spirit. Have fun and avoid getting overwhelmed by perfectionists. Being able to enjoy the process and connecting with your family and friends when you create isn't something you often enjoy, so you should take advantage of it by taking a break and having a great time.

Chapter 3: How To Save On Your Wedding Food & Cake

The choices you have at your disposal for drinks and food is largely depending on the location you've selected. If, for instance, you've selected the hotel, in most instances, they will ask you to make use of their catering services in order to serve your guests. If, however, you have an outdoor venue, you might be able to use catering services of your own.

Choices

In both cases you'll be able to select from a wide range of menus. The venue you choose could charge you more for each additional option that you offer your guests, i.e. generally, two dishes (chicken or fish) are less expensive than three meals (chicken and fish, as well as vegetarian). This is due to it cost those catering services more make the necessary ingredients for three meals instead of two.

Types of Catering

In general, caterers provide different types of food service and. Plated and partially plated, as well as standard buffets and buffets. You can imagine that these are all offered with different prices. It's surprising that a buffet can be more costly than you believe because caterers claim that guests will eat more food at buffets than what they typically receive during a plate service. Therefore, they'll charge you 1.5 to the quantity of food they serve for every guest.

A meal that is partially plated is when a part of the food is served by waiter, but the remainder is served buffet.

The most thrilling type that caters is the buffet-style party. By comparing costs as I considered an outdoor space that would allow catering outside, I realized that buffet stations were similar with regards to cost. They are comparable to almost all other services offered by catering companies , however it all depends upon the supply and fluctuating costs of caterers in the area you live in.

Buffet stations can offer an array of foods for your guests, from macaroni and cheese, or mashed potatoes served in martini glasses, custom-made pasta and barbeque, there's an array of stations for you to select from. This is a fantastic choice if you're hosting an eclectic group of guests of different backgrounds who will appreciate the variety of choices.

DIY

You are able to do your own catering, by enlisting the assistance of your friends and family members. It's a lot more work, however cooking the food yourself can likely save you thousands of dollars on food expenses. Spaghetti or pulled pork sandwiches tacos, lasagna, barbecue meats, turkey, or ribs are all cheap and tasty methods to feast a huge crowd.

When you search "fundraising dinners" or "Inexpensive meals to provide food for a crowd" you'll find many ideas, suggestions, and tips to make your dinner a hit.

DIY Catering Websites that offer recipes and tips

Allrecipes.com-

This page contains step-by-step recipe and directions for making the perfect and delicious spaghetti meal from beginning to end.

Fundraising-ideas.org-

This page is full of diverse "theme" dinner recipes that are simple to prepare for a large group.

HeavenlyHomemakers.com-

Based on their own experiences in cooking for large groups of people. Tips and recipes are extremely useful.

GreatPartyRecipes.com-

This site is designed by people who wish food for a larger number of people. It's packed with tips and charts so that you can know precisely how much you can cook and how much to serve.

Drinks

Similar to catering, the amount of flexibility you have in this sector will depend on the place you've selected. Certain venues are extremely strict and you'll only be able to purchase alcohol through them.If you are in that situation you should inquire to permit you to purchase cheaper wines through their distributors, but with the standard markup. While not ideal, it might save you some dollars.

A majority of restaurants will offer the complimentary champagne toast along with non-alcoholic beverages.

If you're planning to serve drinks to your guests, but are concerned about paying excessively and that's a legitimate issue considering that the cost of an open bar over only a few hours could be as high as $3000, you should consider offering a limited open bar.

A glass of wine, beer or one drink that is a signature drink is plenty to please those with the highest standards and you won't be left with a massive bill at the close.

To get the beer, you can ask the restaurant to offer just a few inexpensive choices and ensure they will cost you for bottles instead of a keg since a keg is more costly. Similar to the wine. A few wine choices with white and red wines is enough to satisfy all preferences.

If you decide to serve the drink as a signature be sure that it's created with low-cost but delicious ingredients.

Visit about.com for a wide selection of cheap and diverse drinks to choose from.

Most importantly, make sure that your venue is aware of your budget for the day and request them to notify you when you're close. The last thing you need to think about on the night of your wedding is how you're going to cover the cost of alcohol that was not within your budget.

If you are able to warn the guests that you are aware, you can create an emergency plan that includes offering fewer options or shutting off the water faucet. However, it shouldn't go this far since your venue must provide an estimate of the budget that is dependent on the number of guestsattending, the number of them will actually drinking and the amount you can anticipate when you pay for the event.

DIY

If you're able to have more flexibility regarding your location (outdoor or in the backyard) you stand a better chance to save a significant amount of money by stocked an in-house bar. Take a look at warehouse clubs like Costco or even stores like Bevmo to find great prices on liquor cases and beers. For wine, there is nothing better than the quality and price of the 3 bucks chuck at the Trader Joes. Get your stock up before the holidays and frequently to ensure you have plenty of wine for guests to select from when they arrive at the wedding.

If you're planning to make the bar yourself, make sure to buy cups mixers, garnishes, mixers and napkins.

You can also use the savings to pay for a bartender or two. You can locate bartenders making use of gigmasters.com and craigslist. You can perhaps asking a friend with experience to manage the bar on your behalf.

Wedding Cakes

Bakery

If you are considering a bakery to bake your wedding cake, the important thing to remember is that you're paying for skilled work and the more skilled labor that you require, the more you'll have to have to pay.

When you are choosing a bakery look up bakeries in your region on the internet first. What bakeries have received good reviews?

Are they trustworthy? Are they around for for a long period of time? Create an inventory of bakeries that you'd like to visit, set up appointments with those bakeries.

Don't just look at traditional bakeries when visiting your local grocery or warehouse shop. Many have talented bakers who will be able to provide an amazing tasty wedding cake for just half the cost of traditional bakeries.

Good bakeries will provide you samples of the various flavours as well as frostings. They will sit down with you and discuss what you would like as well as your budget and provide within these guidelines.

Find out about the various choices available. Are they able to bake and then cover the cake in fondant, and let you decorate it with fresh flowers and save cost? Does the cake come with delivery for free? Are they willing to charge less if they bake many cakes, but do not stack the cakes? This is exactly what we did.

As our wedding was themed, we requested 8 cakes that were inspired by eight different nations. They would be placed in separate pedestals for the cake, decorated just with the same decorations as their countries of origin. meant to represent. Since we didn't require eight cakes for the number of guests Our bakery offered to create two cakes from Styrofoam to help us save costs. These Styrofoam cakes looked like real cakes, and were the perfect solution. We saved quite a bit of money. Our guests could not stop praising our fun variation on the classic wedding cake.

Fake Cakes

Styrofoam cake is a great alternative in order to get the look of a wedding cake with a modern design without spending extravagant costs. The method is that you can purchase or hire an adorned Styrofoam cake and then , when the time comes to serve the cake. The waiters will cut slices of cake from an inexpensive sheet cake that is hidden behind.

In all the wedding noise nobody will be aware of it.

If you're concerned about the formal "cutting of the cake" for your new partner Don't be concerned. A lot of Styrofoam cakes come with a tiny area where you can place a cake to serve this purpose.

Fake Wedding Cake Websites

Fabulous and Faux Wedding Cakes

Ultimate Fake Cakes

Fake Cakes By Catherine

DIY

You or somebody you know is an accomplished baker, this is a possibility to think about. I'd only suggest this if you feel confident about your abilities because this is a challenging task to tackle DIY.

DIY Wedding Cake Websites

MarthaStewart.com

SouthernLiving.com

APracticalWedding.com

Epicurious.com

OffbeatBride.com

As this book continues I hope you're realizing that you are not limited by the narrow perspective and the options the wedding industry has you think you have. There is actually many options when you are planning your wedding on budget. Let's continue exploring these possibilities in Chapter 9 of wedding entertainment.

Chapter 4: How To Save On Wedding Entertainment

After the reception and the ceremony A great wedding reception will be the main aspect of the wedding . What will be remembered for your guests. This is what will differentiate between the "just okay" ceremony and one that is a memorable one.

I've listed a variety of choices below to take into consideration when making a decision on entertainment for your wedding.

Bands

The most expensive choice in wedding entertainment is live bands however it could also be the most enjoyable according to what both you and guests prefer. With prices ranging from $1200 to $1500 per musician for 4 hours of music , it can be quite high.

If you choose to take this option, there are couple of things to keep in mind to ensure you get the most value for the money you spend.

Choosing a Band

What kind of music are they playing?

Contrary to DJs or an iPod the band is limited in the kinds of music they're capable of playing. Are you part of a more homogeneous audience that enjoys big band and classic rock? If yes then a band could be ideal for you.

I was an eclectic mix of Hispanics and German-Americans. Despite the fact that today's bands are more diverse than ever, I would have a tough finding a band who could have been more suitable for our group, rather than DJ.

Have you ever seen them live?

Most likely , the band or bands that you are contemplating playing at are in a range of venues. Go out with your loved ones for an evening of date time and take a look. The bar's setting is distinct from the wedding setting, so be aware of this when you are watching them. Do you like the music choices? Do you have any that you don't like? Are they engaging in the presence of others? Do they appear professional?

What are they offering?

Visit their representatives and get specific questions regarding their services. How many breaks to music are they taking? What do you do when they saw that the guests aren't dancing? Are they engaging with guests?

Do they play different music during the cocktail hour during the meal, and at the dance? Are they able to play the music you plan to use for your first dance as well as additional special occasions? How many musicians should you anticipate? Which instrument will they be playing?

Don't be afraid to speak with a variety of bands prior to deciding to get an picture of what's available there. It is best to begin the process as early as you can, at least six months prior to the wedding date, particularly when you're planning to marry during the peak season.

By arranging your meeting in advance, you'll allow yourself enough time to get to know several bands, and increase the chances of the band you're interested in being at the time you choose to make a booking.

DJ

It's less expensive than live music and my preferred choice can be an experienced DJ. I am awestruck by the variety DJs can offer , and if you locate the right one, they can make the difference between an ordinary party and a memorable one.

Similar to the live band section you'll need to ask a lot of questions to determine the best DJ for your needs. The questions you ask should be similar however with slight differences.

Choosing a DJ

Choose how lively you would like your event to be. There is no need to have the traditional chicken dance and line dancing because you're using DJ.

A professional DJ will have a conversation with you and provide you with many options for your wedding, including the standard songs and games .

Be very cautious about "DJ bridal games". I attended an event where I believe that the bride and groom anxiety that they wouldn't be able to have fun. that they went through every box for games or dances when writing their music papers.

The "dancing" started at 7:15 but the dances were special as well as musical chairs and games which didn't stop until 10:15 at night. We had just 1.5 hours to dance. Many guests were disappointed because of the rules specific to the games, we were to watch the games from the sidelines for the majority of the time because only a few could be "allowed" to take part in the games that were a bit silly.

I would suggest just a couple of special dances. the first one being father-son, and mother-daughter (in my case, mother-daughter). If you've got a lot of older couples married who are in your mirth and you want to pay tribute to them, then the anniversary dance is a lovely one also. That's it. Adults don't need musical chairs, chicken dance or any of the other bizarre games your Dj has in mind to keep them entertained.

What are the genres and songs that you'd love to have included? What are the genres and songs that you'd rather not have? Do you plan to accept guests to make requests? What are the guidelines for this?

Choose your wedding's music timing. Discuss the various choices and possible transitions for the cocktail hour music as opposed to dinner music and dancing music. What time will the DJ be set up? Is it in front of all guests at dinner? If yes, are they capable of setting up earlier?

What's included and what additional features are included with the DJ? Your guests will be looking to make toasts. Does the DJ have a microphone? Do they have special lighting or effects? When will they break? Do they wish to have a meal with the group? What time do they plan to stop playing and go to bed? Do they have the option of playing for an additional hour if they think the event is good? Do they have additional services they provide and what are they?

Where can you find bands and DJs?

1. Friends and family recommendations Ask your family and friends whether they've been to any excellent DJs or bands recently, or if they've been to a wedding reception with an excellent DJ or band.

2. Consider it with your companion - Did you really enjoy that group at the piano bar last

night? The Spanish guitar in The Tapas Bar? Are there any great DJs from your club?

3. Utilize the internet for local wedding message boards on the internet and reviews are an excellent way to locate DJs and bands. Don't limit yourself to DJs or bands in your town. A lot of DJs and bands are willing to travel , so broaden the search area to encompass other cities and areas.

4. Gigmasters- This site is an excellent resource to find top-quality musicians and DJs who have reviews by other people like you.

iPod

The most affordable alternative is to make your own playlist, and act as your personal "DJ". Two of my acquaintances have successfully used this method during their weddings and have saved their weddings a great deal of cash. There are some things to consider before using this method.

Customized Playlists

You can completely modify the music you play at your wedding, which is an excellent and negative thing. You may be thinking what could be negative? If you don't make separate playlists that have similar tempo for different aspects of your wedding, it can cause your wedding to stop from beginning to end.

For instance: The most recent energetic Nicki Minaj hip hop track is followed by Sarah Mclachlan's extremely inscrutable "Eye of an Angel". If a large number fans were dancing they're likely to be pondering about what they should do next.

Plan Ahead

Create a list of the music you would like to play during each phase of your reception - the cocktail hour, the special dances, and the dance.

Make use of an app such as my wedding DJ or a virtual DJ, to ensure that your playlist sounds more professional. These apps let your playlist transition seamlessly between songs, with no interruptions in between.

After you have created your playlists, try them out. Listen to them through when you're cleaning your home, cooking or driving to ensure all is well and functioning correctly.

Plan B

Download your partner's iPod, your laptop , and even a friend's iPod with the same playlist to have multiple devices to use in case one fails.

Be Prepared

Take all devices, cables, chargers and everything else you'll require a few days prior to. Check that all your gadgets are powered. Take an extension cord along with additional cords in case. Don't assume that your venue has the equipment you'll require.

Include your guests

Ask your guests which music they'd like to hear prior to the wedding. They can do this on a no-cost wedding website, or through the RSVP cards. Add these to your playlist. Make sure to keep the "DJ setup" slightly hidden from guests. Ask a groomsman or bridesmaid to run at the "booth".

This will keep people away from screaming for help or even disconnection of your playlist to play their most-loved techno tune.

Follow these suggestions to ensure your wedding is moving forward and offer your guests and you an unforgettable celebration.

Chapter 5: How To Save On Wedding Transportation

Alternatives to an pricey limousine when it comes to choosing the best the transportation option for your wedding.

The most basic and classic is to make use of your automobile. Let the groomsmen dress the car using ribbons, cans and even paint. Complete the look with the famous "Just Wed" sign, and prepare to hear all the sounds you'll hear as you head off on your honeymoon.

Keep your theme in mind

If you're getting married at a farm, make use of an tracker, a carriage drawn by horses or horses when you make your exit.

If you're planning to get married on the river or lake you can use a canoe, or if you know someone who owns an inflatable boat and a canoe, ask them to take you up.

If you and your partner like to ride, then using either a traditional or a motorcycle bike is an excellent method to express your personal style together when you depart while saving money.

If you're having your wedding on the golf course, you can employ golf carts.

Explore your topic with a fresh perspective and think about how you could be able to utilize this to reduce costs when selecting your travel plans.

Additional Options

Explore trolleys, party buses, and passenger vans for transporting your wedding guests or party. They are typically cheaper than the stretch limousine while satisfying your requirements. Certain areas even lease school buses to students which is a great option to those who love the idea of learning or simply love the quirky details.

Wedding Photography

It's one of the most expensive aspects of the wedding, but an important one as when the day has ended, all you'll be left with are photographs and memories to recall your wedding day. However, that doesn't mean you cannot still save a significant amount of cash.

Where can I locate Inexpensive Photographers?

It is worth hiring a photography person or a student who's beginning their own business.

• Check local forums for reviews of prospective photographers who might not be widely known.

* Gigmasters.com has a number of highly-rated, affordable photographers to choose from.

Ways to Save

Contact potential photographers to inquire about their packages and times. Perhaps you only require photographers for a portion of the time or maybe just a few hours to take photographs of the family or wedding celebration. This is an excellent way to save cash.

Discuss photo rights. Most often, the cost of photography is high after the wedding and when purchasing prints. Are they willing to provide you with a CD of the photos in order to create prints on your own? Are they willing to offer great prices?

When hiring a photographer, particularly when you're trying to find the best price , here are some things you must do:

You can meet them face-to-face. You can browse through their portfolio and ask questions, as well as address any issues you might have.

Be sure to like the pictures of them. If not, keep searching, as these are crucial for your family and you in the near future. Don't be disappointed by the wedding photos you took.

Make a plan with your partner. It is possible to include photographs of the most important aspects of your wedding day, such as the venue, dress , etc you'd like to make sure that they capture pictures of. Take pictures of the kind of photography you'd like to use to use for the wedding. Do you want an older-fashioned or documentary style? Making these decisions prior to the wedding is crucial in order to get photos you are happy with.

Inform them about the timeframe of the wedding ceremony and work out the most important elements that they should document.

Have they ever been to this location before? If yes are they aware of what to expect on the wedding ceremony? Do they know if the lighting will be off at a specific moment in the day? If they haven't yet been at your venue(s) and aren't there, would they be interested in visiting them to get familiar with the various issues they could face on your wedding day including dim lighting and other obstacles?

As with all other aspects of the wedding is about using your money and time efficiently now, to save more time and money in the future. the road.

Be clear about your goals and requirements, being on the same page with your partner on these issues as well as establishing a budget and communicating these to the vendors you choose can make you and your loved ones a lot of anxiety on the day of your wedding.

UNDERSTANDING THE INDUSTRY

T

Reminisce back to the time you were just a child learning to swim the very first time. When you decided to go for a swim in the pool the parents would be sure to determine how deep the pool prior to allowing you to take a dip. Why would they do this? They want to safeguard you and prepare you for. Unscrupulous parents would be content to let their kids dive straight into swimming pools without knowing the depth they're in. They could end up putting themselves in danger because they don't know how to navigate these deep water. That's why it's vital for any swimmer who's just starting out to know how deep the water inside the pool. In the absence of this, they put themselves in danger.

The same applies to business. If you're just beginning in your journey to become an entrepreneur it is a clear need to familiarize and get acquainted with the intricacies of your business venture. It is essential to understand the kind of business you're getting into. This is crucial because for one it will ensure that you aren't overwhelmed by the difficulties of the issues that are posed to you. Furthermore, you'll be prepared and establish the foundation that will allow you to attain success in your chosen field. Before you actually begin taking action and implementing your ideas, it is essential to acquire a better and more comprehensive understanding of the game that you're attempting to enter. You're probably keen to begin. There's a fire in you that's raging deep within you, and it's giving you all kinds of ideas about how to run your business. This is a great thing. There are many who don't be able to experience the same passion as you do. That's why it's the kind of passion required to remain committed and committed to your work. But, you need to be capable of channeling that enthusiasm to the right people and locations so that you can achieve success.

Now take all of your enthusiasm into information gathering. There are many things you have to know before you even begin taking your first step. The first thing that you must learn about is the battle that you will be entering. This chapter will provide you with a better understanding of the industry of event planning in general and all associated with it. It is essential to understand that you're in an extremely competitive market with highly competent and skilled players who are determined to be successful in their own way. This isn't only the game you should be researching. Also, you must be aware of the various rivals who try to take over your market share.

This could be a bit scary, but don't be putting off your ambitions at this point. Sure, the world of business is intimidating. However, as the old cliche says, don't allow the fear of being struck out prevent you from participating in the game. The point in this article isn't to or scare you. The purpose for this section is raise you to realities of the situation you're attempting to place yourself in. While optimism is generally an excellent trait when you are starting a business but it shouldn't be blind. It is essential to keep your eyes open to be aware of all the aspects you have to be aware of when starting an enterprise.

To begin with this section, we'll attempt to answer this simple query...

Why Do People Need Event Planners?

The famous motivational and author Simon Sinek said, you must find your purpose. What is the purpose behind this business? What is the reason people need an event coordinator in the first instance? What is the reason you would like to create an event-planning company? Before you answer the questions of what's the who's, what's, when's where'sand how's you must answer the question of why. So, let's dig further into this subject and discover why the society needs event planners in the first instance.

For many people, there's the general feeling of distrust towards professionals and experts. This is why many people choose to DIY or DIY projects. They believe they can do all the things they can by themselves. Many use this method to prove them and others. Others it's about cutting costs and cutting costs. In any case, it's your responsibility as an businessperson to convince people that they require them to have you. It is your responsibility to convince your audience that your role as an event planner is essential. All of this starts by knowing why you are needed in the first place.

You may have discovered at a young stage that you had an aptitude for organizing events and getting people to support one cause or scheme. Perhaps it began in high school in which you had to organize study groups or study sessions with your friends. Maybe, it was in college when you managed fundraisers for charities or another organization you believed in. When you first started in the world of work you were required to plan corporate events such as Christmas parties and other. Within your family, you could be the one to call when organizing the logistics for Thanksgiving celebrations. However, the your event planning might be something that comes easily to you, and you were able to have fun doing the process. This is why you decided to go after this business as an business owner. It's not enough to know the joy and satisfaction that planning events brings. You also have to convince others of the reason the reason you're doing this, too. You must convince your customers why they require your services. If you're in need of a refresher here are a few ideas to stimulate your memory.

People Need Proper Time Management

Time is an infinitely valuable resource. As humans, we all want more time to accomplish more things. But, time is a commodity that none of us can afford to buy barter, trade, extend or negotiate for. Any time we have is the time we need to make use of. That's why it's crucial for us to be making the most of any time is given to us.

When it comes to organizing an event, timing is crucial. There are a lot of moving parts, and it's crucial to ensure that everything is functioning as planned. A coordinator or event planner is the person who makes sure that these factors aren't in too early or late.

People Need Proper Financial Management

Although some people believe that they could save money by letting go from the services of professional event coordinators however this isn't the situation. It's true that there are a few event planners that charge a hefty sum of money to provide their services. But most times, these are the same people who will save their customers from financial catastrophes.

A lot of people do not understand that event planners exist to ensure that their clients have the most perfect event they can without overbudget. When unexpected accidents or disasters happen during the planning of events the event can be extremely expensive for an amateur to compensate for the over-runs. The hiring of an experienced event planner will lower the risk of such incidents happening at all.

People Need PROFESSIONAL Creativity

However, it is a talent that not every person are capable of having. But, to be an event planner to succeed it is crucial to be creative. There are many ways to make your event distinct and memorable. This is the reason it's crucial for event planners to remain creative.

Similar to how people seek graphic designers for logo designs or musicians to create jingles, there is always a need for imaginative artistry in the planning and coordination of events. To create an original and distinctive finished product, it will need the involvement of an artist at the beginning.

People Need Objectives and Metrics to be Met

In any gathering or event there are always goals and metrics that must be achieved. In some instances these metrics can be more abstract. In other cases, the goals are more specific and easily quantifiable. For instance, planning weddings could have objectives which are more abstract. In general, clients simply want to have an event that lets everyone be satisfied and to have an enjoyable time. For events that are more business-oriented or business related, there could be specific outputs that have to be fulfilled. For instance, a fundraiser for a charitable cause might have to generate a certain amount financial earnings to be considered successful.

As a customer or participant at these events, it is extremely difficult to be sure that the expectations and goals are met. The bride shouldn't be required to be the sole one to ensure that everyone at her wedding are having a an enjoyable time. This is what the event coordinators of professional are watching out for.

People Need Professionals to Put Out Fires

In accordance with Murphy's Law, everything that can go wrong , will happen. When it comes to coordination and planning for events expensive mistakes and errors in judgment could lead to disasters for events. These would be prevented by a skilled event planner was employed.

Even when professionals handle the event there's still an opportunity that incidents of nature could cause problems for an event. An event provider could have an emergency, and then decide to cancel the event at last minute. A wardrobe malfunction may occur. The food could result as a result of a freak accident. However the fact that an experienced event planner take care of any emergency will take the anxiety off the shoulders of a customer.

People Need Structure and Expertise

When a client employs an experienced event planner it isn't just hiring a person. They also hire an entire event-organizing machine. In addition to the personal planner or coordinator, they also have with a list of vendors, contacts and other valuable resources that are crucial for an event's success. type of event. Additionally the professional business for event planning would have a well-constructed framework and system in place to ensure that the planning of the event goes as smoothly as it can.

More than any other aspect, the amount of knowledge and experience that an expert event planner provides is bound to be useful to any customer who wants to plan an event of a large scale. In the present day there's plenty of big events.

People Need Peace of Mind

In the end, there's going to be that sense of calm that people are looking for in stressful or stressful situations. It's as if you're playing an basketball match and it's tied, with just a few seconds left in the game. You'd always have confidence knowing that you had a player such as LeBron James, and Michael Jordan on your team to complete the task for you.

This is the type of calm that an experienced event planner can provide to a stressful event. Planning events isn't as simple as many people believe. But, if you hire the best event planner, things can be as simple as 1,2 3, 3.

What Does an Event Planning Business Look Like?

Simply put it can be described as the act of planning the coordination, supervision and executing a plan which involves gatherings of many individuals. Some examples of these gatherings are meetings and trade shows, fairs and conventions, birthday celebrations anniversary celebrations launch openings, funerals, weddings and much more. The most fundamental steps that are involved in planning events include budgeting, mobilizing food preparation, coordination of transportation planning, scheduling and managing risk, theme creation invite guests and permit acquisition as well as permit acquisition.

Planning an event is a thorough and meticulous process that requires intense focus on the details, alertness and the ability to see. When planning any event there are requirements that must be maintained and targets that must be fulfilled. It is the responsibility of the event planner to make sure that everything from the planning phase to the actualization of the event is smooth and efficient.

So, an event-planning business is a separate entity, that is comprised of one person or a group of individuals who have an established procedure and machinery that is that is designed to provide events planning and coordination services to its customers. There are many solo entrepreneurs and single proprietors that provide events planning and coordination independently. However the larger the event in terms of its scope and objectives, the parameters, and impacts and impact, the greater the need for greater event planning machine. There are only a limited number of possibilities that an event planner or entrepreneur could accomplish on their on their own. The more people involved in the event-planning business more potential they have to make an impact.

There are a variety of ways that one could organize an event-planning business. But, there are some key areas of event planning that need specific individuals or persons who are in charge. The fields include like this:

* Theme Design and Decoration

* Logistics and Operations

* Finance and Budgeting

* Lighting and Sounds

* Food and Beverages

* Entertainment

* Graphic Design

* Communications

* Scheduling and Planning and so on.

In the end, the larger the event planning company is, the greater the capacity and potential to manage larger events that require more people. But, it's not to suggest that the larger an event-planning business will be, then the less effective it will be, too. Be aware that there are a variety of events that differ in terms of size and scale. It's about creating a company and then finding a niche you believe you will achieve success in. There's still a demand for event planning that is small-scale as well as coordination. It's likely to achieve significant success in this field.

When you go through the book, you'll find ideas and tips that will help your business's event planning regardless of the size. The fundamental principles are identical. The requirements of a large organization for event planning and a smaller one only differ in the degree of their involvement but not by type. It's all about being able to scale your business according to the appropriate scale to meet the needs of a customer.

The State of the Industry

Contrary to what some might think Event planners are much more than simply organizing events. There are numerous aspects of managing and coordinating events that not many people can even consider. A casual person would never imagine the difficulties that come with obtaining permits or coordinating transportation and accommodation. But, the nature of the work done by the event planning industry is mostly on their specialties or areas of expertise. There are a few firms that focus on a few particular areas, while there are other companies that have a greater range of offerings and clients. However, the whole business can be reduced to two distinct market segments that are the Business/Government market and the social market.

The Corporate/Government Market

Based on data from according to data provided by the Event Marketing Institute, the market for event planning and co-ordination is as popular and active in the present as it ever been. According to data published in 2012, businesses tried to increase their marketing budgets for events by as high as 7.8 percent. The blog for event marketing Bizzabo claims in its study that between 2017 and 2018the number organizations that plan at twenty events per year has increased by as high as 17 percent (2018). Bizzabo has also stated that in 2018 the most successful companies are investing 1.7x more funds than the average company to marketing events. Event Marketing Institute Event Marketing Institute has also stated that of the companies which they surveyed 83% of those who responded believed the events had more success in selling than in promoting awareness.

In the age of the digital age the importance of event marketing has increased. Around the globe marketers are using different channels on social media to communicate with their online customers and influencers of brands. In the process, increasing numbers of events are getting massive attention and success because of the coverage on social media. In fact, 66% of participants to this Event Marketing Institute survey have stated that social media has made their events more memorable and effective in terms of impact and reach.

In recent times increasing numbers of customers are responding to strategies being used at government and corporate events. It's evident when campaigners hold rallies or fundraisers in order to get more votes and more financial ammunition to win elections. Businesses participate in trade shows and conventions to promote and endorse their services, products, as well as their brands, to an larger crowd. A growing number of people are taking advantage of these interactive and inclusive activations for brands which allow them to feel a brand's presence up close and in person.

Here's a list that includes the top frequent public or private events:

Brand launches

* fundraisers

* rallies for the campaign

* Conventions

* seminars, etc.

The Social Market

The market for social events might appear like it is a sports event at a lesser scale but it is still making up a large portion of the overall market. This is where the majority of small or solo event-planning firms are capable of finding their market. Actually this is the place the area where the market is the most competitive. The returns and margins may not be as large however, all that is covered by the volume of demand. It is important to note that every day, people are celebrating an anniversary, birthday or wedding, retirement celebration or even funerals. Although these celebrations may seem smaller than events for political or corporate gatherings but they're not only seasonal. They happen regularly regardless of the season. Thus, there won't be a shortage of buyers in this market.

An In-Depth Analysis of the Market

Before you start your business for event planning it is crucial to do a thorough and complete analysis of the market before you integrate it into your business strategy. You don't want to shoot yourself in the foot with setting your sights too high or low. Set realistic expectations for your company and yourself according to the data you collect. Naturally, you'll want to create as many fans as you can in order to grow your business. It is recommended that you set goals for your business as far as extending your fan base is involved. Naturally, this amount may vary depending upon your goals in business. There are a variety of businesses that have achieved significant growth through specialization, which is only one specific market segment or business and sticking with the same niche. There are companies that plan events and have achieved success through being flexible and accommodating to all kinds of needs and niches in the market.

Beyond mastering the art of planning events as well as coordination, you should be aware of the specifics of the market you're aiming to serve. If you'd like to be a part of the sport of political rallies and fundraising then you must be aware of the fundamentals of politics. If you wish to develop the trust of corporate clients, you must be familiar with corporate issues. That's what it is to study and understand the market you want to target.

Looking to the Future

Also, as was earlier mentioned, being aware of the present isn't the only thing you require to achieve success as an event organizer. It is also important to be able to see the future and have the insight essential to know where the industry will go and discover what you can do to adapt your company and yourself in order to remain relevant to the customers that you're trying serve. This is why it is important to keep looking forward to the future, even while trying to stay ahead of all that's happening in your field in the moment.

Everyday, new technologies continue to influence the way humans perform in their daily lives. One way in the way technology has revolutionized the game is in human interaction. Nowadays, we have the ease of being capable of communicating and interacting with other people instantly without having for being present in the same space as each other. This is why events are more important than ever. A gathering that requires people to meet people in the same space must be an experience that surpasses the online interaction and interactions.

In keeping with the constantly changing global nature at large Here are some events industry trends you may want to familiarize yourself with in the near future.

Value-Added Functionality and Versatility

The notion of utility and function is becoming well-known in the present. Indeed that more and more people are becoming more aware about the benefits of a product as well as how they can get the most of it. That's why the latest phones are packed with a variety of functions that let it perform x, y and Z. In the realm of real estate and housing it is becoming increasingly common for people to make the most of small space and utility. This is the case for events too.

Each item associated with the running of an event must serve a specific purpose. This increases the worth of the item along with the event an entire in the eyes of the participant. This isn't solely about adding value to an element or feature. It's also about maximising the value of that feature by making it adaptable. For instance, a popular element for any event is ID card or name tag that are hung from lanyards or necklaces that hang around the neck of an individual. One way to make the most of this small piece of equipment is to include the date of the event on the reverse of the name tag to allow the person to refer to as a source of information.

This way, you're giving more value and utility to an otherwise unimportant event function.

It's not only a way to advertise yourself as cool or trendy. It is a way to show your customers and other attendees at the gathering that you're attentive to the finer details. If you can show your customers that you're willing to take a step back and examine the way events are conducted with events, it will be beneficial to you. The amount of gratitude you show to your client's event will only be able be reflected in the amount of gratitude your clients will show you in the return.

Diversity and Creative Thinking

The world is becoming more accepting of diversity regarding beliefs opinions, thoughts, and ideas. Today, in the digital age people are more eager to learn about opinions which don't necessarily align with their personal views. Event planners need to take advantage of this trend to bring a feeling the diversity of their events. But, it is important to be cautious when it comes to things like this. It is very easy to make people turn off towards the concept of diversity when you attempt to force it in their faces.

Many event organizers try to bring the diversity of their events regards to the participants who attend the attendees. For example, if the event is an event for corporate or business conference, to encourage diversity, event organizers must demonstrate their creativity through a wide range of speakers. Diversity shouldn't only be viewed through the lens of race or cultural background. Think of diversity as a result of the area of specialization or the field of work.

If it's a conference for business made up of firms that are in the financial sector, it is possible to add variety to the event could require an expert keynote speaker whose expertise is in a different field, such as the arts or technology. In this way, you will have an array of diverse ideas which can be debated throughout the whole conference.

While this could be something that is risky however, many believe that it is worth the risk.

Many people are discovering value in new concepts or systems of belief which they're not familiar with. Additionally, adding variety to an event is a fantastic opportunity to make things interesting and break out of the routine.

Mindfulness and Immersion

In case you've not paid attention to popular culture or other mainstream trends, ideas like mindfulness and being present are prevalent these times. It's a bit ironic that in this age of social media, when we are inundated with distraction than ever before, people are beginning to become more aware of the places they are in and what they're doing at any given time. This is the reason that activities such as meditation and mindful breathing are beginning to get popular. There is a fundamental desire for individuals to remind themselves to be focused in the present moment they are. This is supported by specialists in this field who claim that these time periods of relaxation that are provided to the mind are helpful to productivity and creativity.

If you're coordinating an event that demands a lot of output from the participants, you may be thinking about incorporating mindfulness and wellness principles into the way you plan your event. For traditional events, coordinators and planners typically try to pack the most activities and discussions into the timeframes as they can. Although all this may enhance the energy for an occasion, it could also be extremely exhausting, and the attendees could be overwhelmed with everything.

Therefore, as we move towards the future is essential organizers maintain wellness and mindfulness in their minds. This is particularly important when the events are driven by output which means one of the primary measures is productivity. There is a wealth of research that shows that a tired mind is not productive. It would be in everyone's benefit when events paid more focus on the mental health of the participants.

Personalization

Personalization isn't necessarily an emerging or new trend, but it's certainly one that's going to continue to the next. When it comes to analyzing and evaluating massive events, it can be easy to refer to participants in terms of numbers or figures. While these kinds of statistics can be crucial to determining the viability the event has, they do not necessarily reflect the full picture. It is still worth making sure that the organizers acknowledge and respect the uniqueness of the people taking part in these types of events.

But, providing a personal event management is not just about adding a participant's name to the communications and in giveaways. There should also be an element of originality in this regard. Here are some ideas of what could be done to ensure there is an exceptional degree of individualization for your event:

* Always consult. Before the actual start your event you should ask participants about their expectations and how they think the event will unfold. This is an excellent way to determine what your guests are most excited about at the event. Additionally, you can make attendees feel more involved in the event too.

Create an app for your occasion that guests will be able to make use of. They may be able to create profiles of their own and the app can provide personalized services to ensure your event goes well-organized and organized as is possible.

Make sure you think about the giveaways at an event. It's extremely difficult to design custom items for large events. But it shouldn't be too much of a problem for just a small number of guests. In this way, guests feel more taken care of and appreciated. All of these factors contribute positively to the overall assessment of an experience at the event.

Although the primary objective is to ensure certain criteria are being met, it's crucial to acknowledge the importance of a person when evaluating the significance of an incident.

Sustainability

The final trend you should ensure you're in line with is sustainability. There is no need to get involved in all the political aspects of climate change or global warming. This book isn't the right avenue to do that. But, it's foolish to believe that environmental issues aren't crucial to people today. Event organizers are crucial to take these issues into consideration whenever planning events. This is particularly true if the event is eco-friendly and environmentally sustainable. For instance, it could be a fund-raising event to support a climate change awareness group or an event that focuses on the negative consequences caused by global warming. Whatever the reason the more event planners are adopting a more sustainable approach by using sustainable methods and strategies.

One excellent way to be more sustainable when organizing events is to eliminate printed brochures or printed materials. A lot of event planners are doing these days is creating electronic information packs that are accessible via emails or QR codes. Making the transition to digital information distribution is proven as more productive and efficient as eco-friendly. Other options include the usage of compostable cup in place of plastic ones or informing everyone to make use of water bottles and tumblers that are reusable containers.

Sustainability and environmental awareness to a new level at events may also influence the preparation of food and beverages. A good idea is to make any leftover food that is left over from the event given to a charitable organization. Maybe, the food provided at the event needs to be sourced sustainably. These are only a handful of suggestions, but they could be a huge help in making an impact on the participants.

Different Careers Involved in Event Planning

If you would like to excel at planning events, then you need to build a highly flexible and adaptable skillset. As has been stated that there are many aspects of event planning. Being a part of an event-related business implies you must be aware of these various aspects to succeed. In actuality the business of planning events in general has evolved into an extremely complicated and intricately woven industries around the globe. There are many jobs associated with this field, and if you wish to be an effective business manager it is essential to learn about all of these professions.

Event Planner

Of course, there's the event organizer. It is the person in charge of all the work performed in order to make sure that the event is successful. the event. Most of the time, only those adept at multitasking are those who be successful event organizers. Everybody knows that events differ in terms of size, degree of composition, theme and season. This means that there are various types of event planners available. Some are specialized in specific occasions only. For instance, certain event planners are only able to handle weddings while others specialize in corporate events. There are other event planners who are more flexible and possess more expertise. In any case the event planners are the most important person in the successful running of events. They oversee the day-to-day activities and coordination to ensure everything goes according to plan. If there are any emergency situations Event planners are those who have to be on top of things.

Wedding Planner

You may be thinking about why wedding planners are being omitted from the list. The reason wedding planners merit their own place on this list in comparison to other types of planners for events is the fact that weddings are the largest of all. There is no guarantee that everyone will require or have a requirement for an event planner from a company although corporate events are more extensive in size and carry greater stakes. It is not the case that everyone is going to require political or charitable fundraising. However, a large majority of people will to be having weddings. This is the reason why that wedding business is an enormous one. There is a large need for weddings.

To be a professional wedding planner, you must possess all the capabilities as described in the section on an event planner. There is however an extra-specialized approach to be taken. A wedding planner must know about everything that there is to know about certain wedding-related topics like dresses, cakes, decorations, entertainment, venues, religious beliefs, marriage certificates/licences, photographers, videographers, catering services, and guest lists among other things. The most effective wedding planners will already have a list of contractors and suppliers ready for their clients prior to the initial meeting.

Event Space Manager

Event space managers, also known as the venue manager is responsible for everything related to the location where the event is going to be held. They are the ones who are knowledgeable and skilled about the management of their facilities and venues to ensure that the event runs exactly as it can. Venue managers are hosts for a variety of various spaces such as theatres, concert halls ballrooms, convention centers arenas, and other similar venues. They are aware of the design, layout, and atmosphere of their spaces, so they can make these information accessible to their customers should they require it. When planning an event, having understanding of the venue is essential. There are a lot of errors in logistics that can be a consequence of a lack of knowledge about a location.

Sponsorship Coordinator

They don't normally come to the forefront for personal events like birthdays, anniversary celebrations, or weddings (although they have been involved occasionally). Most often, they are the kind of people needed to coordinate commercial, corporate or political events that require substantial funding or financial support. To succeed as a successful and effective sponsor coordinator, you should have excellent interpersonal capabilities. It's also beneficial to have a large list of sponsors that are available or if they are persistent and able to find these sponsors. A prime example of why a coordinator for sponsorships needs to be in place can be when a not-for-profit is planning to hold an event to raise funds. A sponsorship coordinator is in charge of ensuring that the non-profit organisation would have enough funds to hold the event in beginning.

Catering Services Manager

Food. There is no way to deny that it's important to serve quality food served at an event. In fact, lots of people believe that bad food can cause chaos to even the most organized events. This isn't just about eating food that tastes great. It's about also ensuring the safety and health of all guests who attend the occasion. If there will be guests who require special food items due to an allergy or other reasons, the catering service manager must be aware of it. Most of the time managers in catering services must possess basic cooking abilities and know-how about cooking and food preparation.

Social Media Manager

Today social media has influenced the entirety of daily life. The event industry isn't immune to the growing influence of social media. In every country individuals are using social media as a powerful instrument for communication and marketing even for their own events. Couples are planning Facebook events to build their guest lists as well as RSVP platforms. Corporates will use Instagram to promote their brand launches or events. However, it could be a major issue if the messages on social media aren't well-defined, consistent or properly designed. The social media administrator steps into the picture. It is the responsibility for the manager of social media to ensure that the content posted through social media in connection with the event is planned and properly executed.

Staff Coordinator

In order to successfully execute an event, an event organizer will need to be able to manage the different individuals who are in their employ. For instance, for corporate events, event planner may need employ ushers to ensure guests are in the right place when they are required to be. The supervision of ushers and usherettes will be under the direction of the coordinator of staff. This person ensures that all employees are performing their duties effectively and completing their tasks efficiently. A staff coordinator person who is responsible for ensuring that all the components of the machine function according to the specifications.

Communications Manager

Then, there's the communications manager, or marketing manager of the event. This position is crucial in events that incorporate any kind of branding or marketing element to them. For instance when a corporate event intends to announce a new item or service, it's the responsibility that the communication manager make sure there is a solid foundation for collaterals as well as documents associated with this new product are efficient and functioning properly. An excellent example would be for a company that offers video gaming to create a variety of gaming booths during an event so that guests can play these games in person. It is the responsibility of the marketing or communications manager to ensure that the booths are marketing or conveying the real spirit of the product being presented.

Final Thoughts

There are some who believe that the most efficient and efficient event planner is one who is able to wear many roles. However, that's not always the scenario. Actually, there's an argument that the reverse is true. A planner for events who wears many different hats and is accountable for many things will not always be the most effective. Be aware that individuals are able to only accomplish the things they can by themselves. Instead, the most effective kind organizer is one who is aware of the numerous layers and the complexities that are required to ensure that an event is successful. Instead of trying to manage everything by themselves, they partner with the best team to complete the task.

This is a highly complicated one. It's getting more complicated each day, as event planners continually pushing their creativity and bringing fresh ideas into the mix. I hope that this chapter will give you a deep knowledge of the condition of the industry as well as the direction it may be headed. There is a possibility that the information provided in this chapter could become outdated within five or 10 years. That's why you should be proactive and ensure that you are taking every step possible to maintain a eye on the business that is going on around you. As you get more familiar with how things are conducted in the world of event planning and gain an in-depth insight into how you place yourself in the grand plan of the game. The important thing here is you ensuring that you've got a solid strategy for your entry into this market.

ESTABLISHING A FOUNDATION FOR YOUR BUSINESS

I

In the last chapter, you had an insight into the world that you're trying to enter and become an element of. Hope that the knowledge you gained from that chapter didn't take you off just but. Don't worry. Although the business may be tough as well as competitive and daunting, it does not mean there isn't an opportunity for you to make it. This chapter will guide you in forming your strategy to establish your own business for event planning. Be aware that setting up an enterprise in any field isn't something you can simply do at the whim of a. It's going take lots in planning, dedication and hard work by your side to ensure that everything goes to the most optimal outcome. But, even then, it's not always the case that you'll to be in the position you'd like to be with regard to your goals in the field.

This section, we're going to take an in-depth review of the initial steps you must follow to begin earning your first dollars in this business. We'll go over the fundamentals like knowing and understanding your market, selecting your area of expertise, creating teams, as well as everything in between. It may seem like you've got plenty of work to do but that's simply the nature of being successful. You won't reach where you'd like to be if you're not prepared to work hard. But, in addition to the effort, you have to establish a solid strategy. The book will not assist you much in terms of effort and motivation. It's something you need to be looking for. What this book will aid you in is direction and a strategy.

There is no need for to have a bachelor's degree and years of postgraduate study in order to be successful in the business world. Naturally, it's possible that you could be able to benefit if you have a formal business education. However, that won't be an absolute requirement. There are many people who have achieved success in business with little or no formal training. But, this doesn't mean you should not have the intellect and spirit of a student. You must still adopt the mindset that of an academic. There's a lot to be learned and you should keep your mind open to new ways of thinking and ideas. of thinking.

But, before we move on to the main point of the chapter you should understand that it's fine to not be in agreement with everything discussed in this chapter. If you feel that certain ideas or methods don't fit your needs and you're not sure why, that's fine. What is important is to find an approach that is beneficial to you and gives you the best outcomes. Do not be afraid to think outside the box and trying out your method a at times. That being said the best advice for starting your own company would be to follow that...

Get Certified

It is a fact that the world of event planning is full of players who want to challenge one another and capture the largest part of market. Everyday new companies and entrepreneurs popping up , and all of them believe that they will be the next big thing in event management. Therefore it is essential to make every effort to ensure you have a competitive advantage over your competitors. One way you can be ahead of the rest of your peers is to go through the credible certification programs that are readily available.

Different Kinds of Certification Programs

There are a variety of certification programs that provide extensive support, training and accreditation to anyone who is serious about planning events. It's certainly not mandatory to take part in these certification courses. They cost quite a bit of money and are often time-consuming. It's totally acceptable to go on working without the need to be certified. But, there are many who believe that the benefits of taking your time required to be certified are astronomical and certainly worth the investment. If you're wondering the kinds of certifications offered to you, below is an overview of the most notable ones.

Online Event Planning Certifications

Where can people go when they need anything, any thing these days? The internet. It shouldn't be an unwelcome surprise to anyone that you'll be in a position to use the internet to get a certification to plan an event. This is the ideal method for novice or new event planners looking for an efficient and simple method to get a certification. There are a myriad of online certifications appearing everywhere. It's crucial to be careful about the type of certification you're receiving and whom you're getting it from. It's not a good idea to be paying a lot of money and time for a certificate that has nothing of worth within the actual world. While online certifications are generally considered to be less expensive methods of getting certificates, they can be very expensive too. Online certifications for event-related planning be between $50 and $300 dollars. Note that the most expensive certificate isn't always the best or most highly regarded one.

If you decide to go this route to obtain the certification, you must ensure that you're very careful and conduct your due diligence. Make sure to check the history of the company you'd like to get the certification from. Don't be hesitant to ask any seasoned event planners you may know about their experiences and opinions on the subject.

College/University Courses

If the world of online isn't your thing You can earn your certification in the traditional method: by attending school. If you do some searching, you'll find a local institution or university that has events planning certifications. A few schools provide degree programs solely based on the planning of events. But, it's probable that many schools will offer short courses or specific professional certification programs in this area. In addition to the knowledge that you obtain from these schools be beneficial to your practice, but they could assist in building your credibility and reputation as a professional in the area.

Similar to searching in search of an on-line certification provider, you need to be cautious about the school you decide to join. You must look into their history and research the curriculum in depth. Of of course there are many advantages to attending an accredited school and following a legitimate academic program. But, it's not an option that is the best budget-friendly choice for the majority of people. It's expensive to go to school. The process of obtaining a certificate from a school or college ought to be viewed as a type of capital investment.

Event Planning Association Certifications

In terms of discussions of accreditations for event planners You must be familiar to this Certified Special Events Professional (CSEP) certification. This certification was created in 1993 in order to honor experts in the field of event planning by demonstrating their abilities, expertise and ability to offer high-quality event coordination services. Alongside being awarded the CSEP designation, there's an official Certified Meeting Professional Certification issued by the Events Industry Council and the Certified Meeting Planner Certification issued by Meeting Planners International. In terms of certifications related, they are considered to be the holy trinity within the world of event planning. If you can receive these certifications you've established your position as a genuine participant in the industry. The most significant benefit of getting these certificates is they enhance your reputation and brand name as an event organizer. But, the main drawback is that they aren't simple to attain. They will take a significant amount of effort and time for you. Additionally it is true that these programs could be very costly. If you decide to pursue this option it is essential to be ready to cash an enormous check.

The Argument Against Getting Certified

So far, we've identified the benefits of spending the time and spending the money to become certified in the world of event planning. Let's now look at the flip aspect of the issue. Do you really need you to become certified or is the hassle worth it?

Let's say you're new to the field, and you're driven to make an income from organizing events. You're prepared to go through whatever you can to complete the task however, you must be sure you're spending all your time and money into wise investment and assets. You are aware that the expenses of getting certified can be quite high. You know that it can greatly benefit your career however you're not certain that you'll have to go through something similar to this. What should you do?

In this digital age all the information you need to conduct an event successfully is available for you to access via the click of a Google search, isn't it? Why should you enroll yourself in a program to earn certification when you can find these courses on the internet for no cost? If this is a thought that you are having currently it is important to be aware that they are legitimate points. There are many event experts who say that you don't actually need a certificate to be successful in the field. Actually, there are some who argue that getting a certification isn't guaranteed success in your business. It won't instantly guarantee you a job in an event company. All of these are true, and have a lot of significance.

The most important argument you could make to stop getting certified is that experience-based knowledge is likely be much superior to theoretical knowledge. This is different when learning sponsorship, marketing coordination and logistics classroom in contrast to being at the ground and being in the field.

This doesn't mean that knowledge from a theoretical perspective is ineffective. There will always be value in completing an educational program designed to be structured and can help you prepare to be ready for the real world. The main thing to remember is that, while certification programs are efficient tools to prepare however they will not be required to get a job in this field.

Initial Expenses

Nowis the time to address an extremely sensitive subject particularly for young entrepreneurs or businesses that are just starting out. It's time to discuss the financial aspect of a business. This is the main reason for starting a business in the first place isn't it? You're not trying to set up a charity which provides the event planning and coordination service without any reimbursement. You're looking to establish an actual enterprise that is capable of supporting your life. You think you could make use of your talents and skills to establish a lucrative business that can help you pay the bills and climb upwards in the business ladder. However as the maxim goes:

you have to make investments to earn more. This chapter will focus on instructing you on how to structure your business according to the initial investment and financial system.

If you're someone with plenty of money to burn, then this will not matter to you. This means you'll have some room to play and experimentation. But, if you're not fortunate enough to have unlimited resources, or don't enjoy playing with a large amount of money, then you must be careful regarding how you spend the money you have to begin an enterprise. It begs the question: how much will you have to shell out to establish an event planning company? The answer? It depends.

Of course the answer to this question isn't clear and dry. There are many variables and variables to be considered when deciding on a budget. In order to help you get a rough idea for the amount you'll need to spend We will discuss several of the major aspects of business that you must be considering when creating your budget plan.

Rent

The cost of renting will vary greatly based upon the scale of your company and the scope of your business. On the lower end range, it's possible that you might pay no cash to rent if you're working from your personal house. However, this could not be an option which is accessible to larger operations that require a huge team and a variety of departments. There are companies that plan events who will offer between $2,500 and $3,000 per month to rental.

Equipment

In contrast to renting, you're not likely to have the luxury of not spending money for the equipment you need in your business of planning events. In order for your clients to respect your business it is essential to ensure that you dedicate some money towards high-quality equipment you can utilize to host your events. The first step is to should ensure that you purchase the necessary technologies for communication, such as tablets, smartphones, laptops and desktop computer. In the next step, you should purchase the typical operational and logistical equipment including pen and printers, tape clipboards, and so on. If you're determined to become a more comprehensive company for planning events, you can also invest in more sophisticated equipment such as tables chairs, chairs and lighting fixtures, stage equipment as well as photo booths and much more. If you're on the low part on the scale, you can expect to pay approximately $5,000 on basic equipment. If you're seeking to truly fill out your event, you could look at a total cost of up to $20,000 for your event equipment.

Licenses and Taxes

Another cost that your business for event planning won't be able to stay away of is bureaucratic red tape you must go through in conjunction with the government. Naturally, when wish to establish your company as a legitimate business entity, you'll have to get all the required permissions, permits and licences issued by the federal government. In the absence of this, you could end up being a rogue business and make your business an illegal. While it's not easy dealing with the authorities at times however, it's a requirement that you, along with all other business owners must be able to. Based on the location you reside in along with the amount of business it is possible to pay about $200-$400 to get your permits and taxes.

Communications

Communications are essential in the event that your company is likely to consist of many departments or individuals. You must invest in communications and technology which enable you to easily communicate with each other in a group. Without the proper communication lines the synergy of your company's effectiveness could be severely affected. Examples of communication expenses are telephone bills, internet charges, platforms for communication, and much more. In general, companies spend between $100-$300 a month on communications expenses.

Salary/Payroll

In addition to rent, salary are often considered to be the biggest recurring expense of any company. This is especially true when you're running a massive business that employs a large number of employees. Of course, you could be able to reduce your initial salary costs by having no other employees apart from yourself. If that's the scenario, you'll be totally restricted by the things you can accomplish by yourself. If you really want to keep it simple to begin your own business however, you are able to choose to not pay yourself first a salary. However this is only an option if have enough money saved to ensure that you are able to continue operating until the business is profitable. If, however, you're employing others in the beginning, you can expect to spend a significant amount of money to ensure they stay on board. There are several large and medium-sized beginning event planning firms with payroll costs that can amount to up to $5,000 per month.

Advertising

The process of establishing your company's operational structure and putting together your team is only the beginning. It is essential to let your customers know that you are there and that your products are accessible to them. Yes, you could start your business the traditional method of relying on old-fashioned advertising. But, you'd be restricted by your personal network using this method. To reach markets that are outside your reach, it is necessary to utilize advertising platforms. It is only the best way you can make sure that people truly hear about your business. Depending on the scale of your business, the scope, and the size of your promotional initiatives, you must set aside between $300 and $2,500 for promotions every month.

Legal Fees and Accounting

A key element to establishing your business as a legitimate and trustworthy business is to ensure that all financial and legal matters are properly addressed. If you are a lawyer or have a lawyer friend, then you'll cut out the cost of having to employ an attorney dedicated to managing your company's legal affairs. This can also be said for those who are an accountant certified. You may be the one who oversees your accounts to ensure all your accounts are in order. However, if you're not a lawyer or accountant, you're likely be required to engage one of them. Depending on the person you contact and where you live as well as the scale of your business and the size of your business, you may be paying between $600 to $1,500 in accounting and legal fees.

Insurance

Of course, you'll need to ensure that you are your company safe. You must be realistic and accept it is possible that the business won't be able to grow in the manner you'd like it to, or that some events could occur that could cause damage or even compromise to your assets. The right insurance for your business is a crucial part of being a trustworthy and established business owner. You'll always need that security net in the event of a mishap. Depending what the dimensions of your company and the location you are in the cost could range between $500-$2000 for basic insurance.

Miscellaneous

Finally, there are various costs. These are expenses that you won't be able to put into one category or category. They include the cost of meetings with clients, small office maintenance expenses, cash top-ups and many other. In the case of miscellaneous expenses, it's recommended to budget an amount of at least $500 per month, when you're beginning your company.

Building an Operational Framework

If you're considering setting up on the market your own event-planning company, it's unlikely that you've an ordinary 9-to-5 job that consumes the majority part of the time. In reality, the requirements of the creation of an event planning company will far exceed the requirements of the typical 9-to-5 workplace job. As an event organizer, you will need to be available all day, including weekends, weeknights and on holidays too. Based on the niche you are in and the size of your business you may be working every day of the year. Certain event companies are restricted by their industry and may have seasonal operations. However, it is not possible to operate during normal working hours. There are no restrictions to the schedules in the field of event.

Because of the lack of structure in the time and schedule that you work in, there's an unavoidable need to automatize and streamline the other aspects in your enterprise. You aren't able to completely be in control of the hours you work but you are able to decide how you manage your work. Naturally, methods and procedures can vary depending on the event coordinator. But, if you're new to the field and don't know how to structure your plan, here's an acceptable format that you can use to get going:

Preliminary Research and Investigation

Do your homework. Don't enter an encounter with guns without having weapons. You must be prepared by conducting a thorough study and research into the field and market you're targeting. Examine the trends that are currently affecting the world of event management in the present. Conduct surveys as needed and hold focus group discussions you might need to conduct to get an understanding of an event you're planning. Get in touch with other coordinators and event planners and discuss their methods and methods of planning specific events. Find the top contractors and suppliers you can use to help you with the project you're working on. The final and most important element that you should be looking into is to have complete communication with your customer about their expectations and needs. When it comes down to it the client will turn out be the primary participant in this process. In this regard, you should be sure to listen to them and learn what they are looking for from you professionally. This is the work you'll need to complete for your client to ensure that you are able to bring their vision to reality.

Event Design and Conceptualization

Once you've completed all the due diligence as well as initial consultations now is the time to begin creating, drafting and conceptualizing your event along with the team. If you're a innovative person, then this is where you'll be able to show off your skills. Based on your research and the information you've collected and gathered, you now need to create an outline of what the occasion is likely to be like. If you've got a team that you work with ask them to share their ideas too. While you're planning your event, you should to conduct research periodically to make sure the plans you have in place are feasible and in line with your research.

Proposal Draft and Presentation

After you've come up with a strategy and layout for your occasion, you're now able to draft your plan and present it to your customer. In this stage it is crucial to be able to keep your expectations in check. While you've invested lots of effort and time in imagining an event, don't assume that your client is going to instantly be happy with your plans and concepts. Expect some clapbacks and disapproval from your client and ensure that you're not upset by anything. Be aware you are the biggest person in the process, and their opinion is crucial. Don't be scared of imposing a charge on a client in this particular phase. You've used up lots of time and effort to come to a proposal presentation. It's a common practice for businesses that are in the business to charge for initial consultations , regardless of whether the client opts to push ahead or no. If your client wants some minor changes to your strategy, listen to them and adjust to their preferences. You are able to offer suggestions and suggestions based upon your knowledge. However, you shouldn't impose your opinion on them. Be friendly and professional.

Organization and Preparation

Should you and your guest come to an agreement about your proposal for the event and its design the next step is to begin making the first preparations for the foundation for your event. This is when you begin booking venues, securing contractors, and making contact with suppliers. Much of the work in this stage involves calling and arranging appointments or scheduling slots with individuals. This process can be made simpler when you employ employees who get paid to complete this for you. If you're forced to complete this task on your own, be prepared to have many conversations with various individuals. It's not enough to simply hire these suppliers or contractors. You must ensure that they're doing all they must accomplish in order to be prepared for the event. This means that you must keep track of regular progress and follow-up reports. This is the time when much of the labor-intensive work happens.

Coordination and Management

When the event it's just an issue of execution. If you've performed your work well in the earlier phases and you've done most of the job. But, as the saying says, the job isn't done till the big lady starts singing. There's a possibility that certain expectations will not be met in the event itself. This is the reason you have to be on top of all the right gears. As an event planner you must be on guard by ensuring that everyone on your team are performing the things they're supposed doing. Imagine your event as a film and you're the director who has everyone in the right direction. If there are any emergencies or complications that occur, you must be ready to handle the situation and ensure that the entire event isn't affected.

Assessment and Evaluation

The fact that the event has ended doesn't mean that the work is done. As a planner you have the opportunity to review and evaluate the event in a comprehensive way. This is crucial for your customer as they must feel confident that you have fulfilled all your obligations and responsibilities in a satisfactory manner. This is also essential for your staff because you can use it as a chance to pinpoint possible areas for improvement when you continue in your company. Beyond ensuring that there was a successful event it is also important to ensure that the event was evaluated through objective eyes. The feedback you collect from an event doesn't have to be internal. In order to go over, consider getting feedback from the outside stakeholders of the event too. This can provide you with a deeper and rounded view of the events that was conducted.

Generating Income

Money is important. Cash flow is an important element of operation that it has its own section that has to be studied in depth. It is possible to employ a bookkeeper or accountant to assist you in managing the cash flow. But, as an entrepreneur and proprietor of a business, it's vital that you keep at the top of all the money flowing through as well as out of the company. When you become aware of the cash that's going through your event-planning company, you will be able to gain more insight into how you can be pricing your business as an business owner.

The standard rule of thumb is to implement a markup on your labor costs and also on the cost of your supplies. The markup must be substantial enough to cover the overhead expenses your company has incurred. However it should act as the basis for making your business financially viable. There are a variety of entrepreneurs and proprietors who have made the error of pricing themselves too low to lure customers and customers. While this may be a viable marketing strategy to attract customers however it's not sustainable in the long run to run an enterprise. Based on the recommendations of a variety of experts in the field how you rate yourself and your services will depend on the following factors:

The Target Market

In the beginning, you have to determine your market. How you price your products and products will largely depend on the client base that you want to please. Naturally, based on the type of event you're conducting, your pricing is always going to differ. If you're hosting an event that is social and you need to engage suppliers, vendors or contractors, you'll typically need set a price for your services, in addition to the percentages that your other participants would be paid. If you're managing an event that is corporate and you're responsible for managing everything, it's fine to offer an increase for every contract you sign. As an example, you may hire a florist from another business. As an event planner it is acceptable to pay yourself a markup, or commission on this basis. It's also a common standard for businesses to offer a predetermined budget to event planners , and then you'd be required to design your services to the budget they provide you with.

Geography and Season

Like in real estate, your place of residence will greatly influence the pricing you set for your business. One of the most important factors is to look at the costs of living in the area. If your company has to fund high-cost expenses that are caused through payroll, rent and other expenses, then you'll have to charge a bit higher to make your company more viable and profitable. Additionally, if you reside in an area with a high income that is an excellent reason to raise the cost of your products and services. However when you reside in an area that is relatively low-income and you're not charging too much because the people there won't be able see the value of your services.

Also, it is important to take into consideration the seasons too. When you reach the close of the year, when there are many celebrations for the holidays, you may want to raise the price of your services as the demand for your services rises too. If you own the wedding planning business then you must be aware that summer and spring weddings are very popular, too. When these seasons are in full swing it is important to increase your prices to increase profits. It all depends on the location where your business is located and at what season it is. Also, you'll be required to do your fair amount of research in order to make sure you're setting your prices appropriately in relation to these specific aspects.

Strength and Reputation of the Brand

There's a reason brands such as Patek Philippe is able to charge hundreds or thousands of dollars to purchase a watch and also why brands like Seiko and Swatch only offer watches priced at around 100 dollars in value per watch. They're selling the same device. It's a device that can tell the time. What is it that makes the markup for one brand much higher than the other? It's all in the quality and reputation of the name. There's a distinct feeling of trust, tradition as well as exclusivity, that come from having an Patek Philippe timepiece as compared to Seiko. Seiko. This is the reason why both companies are able to charge quite differently, even though they're selling the same thing that is an electronic watch.

The same applies to your role as an event planner. If you've already made an established and well-known name for your business, then you will surely be in a superior position to charge more than others who may have just started out or haven't earned well-known reputations. If you're new to the field, it's going to be extremely difficult to determine the best way to price yourself appropriately. Of course, the majority of newbies do not charge at a higher price because their customers will naturally opt to more reliable organizers of events or companies that charge a premium. If you're only beginning your journey it is recommended that you remain humble and attempt to market yourself in a competitive manner. Find out your worth and strive to establish yourself as an event organizer first. Offer great services. The more valuable you are as an event planner grows as a result, the more you'll be able price yourself over the long term.

Finding Your Niche

As you've probably read in the earlier chapter the event industry has market which can usually be divided into two types which are: corporate and social. When you talk about corporate events, you're not just talking about other companies or corporations. There are events sponsored by non-profit and political organizations as well as charities and other. These are various organizations or organizations that host events with the aim of expanding their brands to their targeted market. For certain events that are specialized there are certain figures or metrics that have to be fulfilled. These numbers may be in the form of attendance, revenue generated or ticket sales, for instance. In this particular field the special events organized by corporations (and similar organizations) are now very significant to set their brands apart from competitors'.

For non-profit charitable institutions, charitable organisations, and philanthropic organizations events such as galas receptions, fundraisers and tickets-based sporting events are popular. There are thousands of such events happening during the course of the year. Of course, arranging such events can only be a feat suitable for bigger event planning organizations or even businesses. If this is the area that you'd like to be in it shouldn't be difficult to find events in your vicinity which fit within the requirements and scope of your business.

The companies are also involved in the event planning area, which could be an area you are looking to penetrate. There are many organizations that host trade shows that host a variety of microbrands and entrepreneurs to display their products and services to a large crowd. Some companies organize events or seminars that feature keynote speakers as well as learning modules. Corporate events can also be held which are more private in nature, such as Christmas celebrations, corporate picnics, team building events and private gatherings. Because of the variety in corporate gatherings, certain event planners would not extend beyond the realm of managing corporate events only. Naturally, considering the strength of different sectors it is a large market worthy of exploring. However, you must be aware of these warnings. There are a variety of possibilities in the field of corporate planning events. The business of this specific niche will bring you steady revenue and profit margins. However, these events aren't a fun because the stakes and expectations are generally much greater.

This is the reason it's suggested for start-ups or boutique agencies businesses that plan events to focus on social events and develop a sturdy equipment and operating system within this niche before moving into corporate events of a large scale.

Let's discuss the possibility of finding your niche managing social gatherings. If you are talking about social gatherings such as these, they're the types of gatherings that encompass birthdays, weddings and anniversaries and so on. There is certainly less pressure associated with these kinds of events because of the relaxed and fun nature of these events. This is why they are an ideal area for new event-planning companies to look into from the beginning. When it comes to the audience for these types of events is focused, it's people who are in the middle to higher income brackets. These are people who have more money for extravagant events and parties but lack the time or expertise to plan these occasions.

Based on trends that are emerging that show the increasing need for events that involve social gatherings such as birthdays, anniversary celebrations, and weddings is expected to keep growing in the coming years. This means that , even although the planning of events will get more competitive, there's still high demand for these services.

The time is now to be asked: Where do you fit in? What's your specialization?

Whatever area you'd prefer to focus your efforts as an event organizer it is essential that you keep in mind the possibility of going smaller with the scope of your specialization. If you're looking to specialize in very specific events such as birthday parties for kids or celebrations of anniversary do not be afraid to take that route. If you do not choose to specialize in some kind of niche that you are not in, it will be more difficult to enter the industry of event planning overall. It's much simpler for potential customers to locate your company when they discover you. Let's say you are able to establish your reputation as the most sought-after event planner for corporate team building events or events. Therefore, if you know of a small or medium-sized firm in your local area that wants to plan celebration, it's likely to get them in touch with you , as rather than an all-inclusive or general event organizer.

However, it's not all about making yourself visible or distinctive in the marketplace. It's also about making life easier for yourself when you're only beginning your journey. It's much simpler to master one thing in a short amount of time than manage multiple skill sets over an extended period of time. If, for instance, you are a specialist in kiddie party You'd already be acquainted with the typical vendors, contractors and vendors for kiddie party events already. There is a prepared list of clowns, jugglers magicians, bounce houses suppliers, face painters and much more. Naturally, as an event organizer having a list of contractors who are possible candidates is going be an invaluable resource to you as you move forward. Building relationships with these contractors will make the process easier in the end.

Additionally with regards to your capital expenditures it's more straightforward to utilize your money in a wise way by sticking to the specific niche. It won't be necessary the burden of spreading your investment expenses over a large area when you're staying within the boundaries of a particular area of planning events. If we're going to apply the kiddie-party example, you will not require expensive things like LED screens, red carpets, arches software for planning events, and the like, since these aren't things that you typically see at these kinds of parties.

For a brief overview of the possible niches for social events you can get involved in you can refer to the following list:

* Children's Parties

* Gender Reveal Parties

* Baby Showers

* Bridal Showers

* Bachelor's Parties

* Weddings

* Surprise Parties

* Anniversary Parties

* Graduation Parties, etc.

If you're looking to break into the market for corporate events, here are some categories that may tickle your interests:

* Private Meetings

* Corporate Conferences

* Corporate Seminars

* Fundraising Events

* Corporate Retreats

* Retirement Parties

No matter what field you decide to venture into, it's crucial that you conduct some study first. It's a huge mistake to create an industry niche although there's no demand for these services in the particular area of your business. You should research the requirements of the market you want to reach and use any information or data that you are able to collect. For instance, if you live in an urban area, then it is appropriate to go into niches in the field that of business events. If, however, you're operating in a rural location, it might not be the most appropriate option for you as the owner of your business. It might be difficult to find customers for corporate events in a market that isn't in the market for it. In this case, maybe an investment in social events could be more appropriate.

Final Thoughts

There are many entrepreneurs or business proprietors who claim that the most difficult aspect of starting a business is actually beginning it. The initial struggles of starting a new venture are real. However, with time, when you have established an established routine for your own business and yourself it will be apparent that things will flow more easily to you. However, if you're a new business owner, things can seem quite intimidating and scary. It's normal to feel that you're not welcome in the society you're trying to break into. This sort of "outsider" feeling is common for many new entrepreneurs. However, it's all based on your ability to develop the courage and determination to be an entity to be reckoned with.

Entrepreneurship is a job that requires an extremely specific set of capabilities. Additionally being a successful event planner is likely need a specific set of skills in addition. When you move through the world of business it is essential that you constantly commit to developing your abilities. It is essential to always be in the process of learning. Keep track of everything that is happening in the business world surrounding you. Be aware of what is taking place in your business. A part of the stress you are experiencing at the beginning will be typical. You may feel as if you're feeling frustrated because you're not able to pay your bills on time or your company isn't making money. This is normal. There are many businesses that need to wait for many years before they can make any sort of profit. It is hoped that you will not be waiting this long. The important thing here is to be patient and alert. It's not a good idea to make a fuss about it However, you don't want to become complacent either.

It's important to get started, but finding your groove after you have your base established is more crucial. Also, don't get too easily overwhelmed by the many difficulties and obstacles that are waiting for you once you begin an enterprise. It is essential to be immune to these challenges in every way. It's extremely depressing to realize that you're exerting many hours of effort, but you're seeing very little reward. However, if you're constant and persistent for long enough, you'll discover you're reaping rewards bound be forthcoming quickly. It's merely a matter of taking your time in the time being.

BEING AN EFFECTIVE EVENT PLANNER

H

In the event that you've adhered to the guidelines in this book to date it will give you all the basic equipment and processes will allow you to start your journey as a professional, legitimate event organizer. It's now an issue of honing in specific techniques and establishing the right habits to get to becoming a master of your craft. Also, you must be aware that even though you might have good intentions when it comes to serving your customers, you face competition. There are others with similar interests to yours and trying to take market share, too. To remain ahead of the pack, you must be doing all you can to build your business up and ensure that customers are aware of the reasons why they should choose you to provide events planning services.

This chapter we're going to explore the ways to improve your effectiveness and become a proficient event planner throughout your career. Of course, you'll need to recognize that it'sn't only about flawlessly planning an event and thinking that you don't need any other lessons to take in for the duration of your existence. In reality, it's extremely uncommon (almost almost impossible) for a new event organizer to not do something wrong, particularly on the first couple of occasions. If you're trying to make your name within the field it is likely that you will discover a lot about yourself as an event organizer and how you'll be able to fit into the market you're trying to break into. Self-reflection and self-learning are beneficial and is an source of knowledge that you can apply to improve your performance.

Imagine your job as planning an event like an intricate meal you need to prepare. Like any food you prepare there are a variety of ingredients in order to make the food taste better. In this instance making the right recipe to become an efficient event planner requires specific skills and behaviors that you can adopt to make sure you're competent to provide professional services. The better your serviceis, more likely that they will return to you time and again to avail whatever services you have to provide. This chapter will give you the basic recipe you'll will need to create an attractive event planning company. The first step is to note that you don't need to worry too about it if many of the tips listed here do not apply to your situation at this point. There's no way to expect that you'll be an expert in the first few months because you're beginning. Naturally the learning curve always high even when you're an inexperienced. It's simply a matter being aware of all the abilities are required to sharpen and the habits you have to instill in yourself.

Essential Skills of an Event Planner

Although it's satisfying to work on something you're interested in for an income however, it can be extremely stress-inducing. You are probably one who is a great event planner and that's the reason you've chosen this career path in your life. But just because you are enthusiastic about something doesn't guarantee that you'll be completely free of any anxiety or stress. Many experienced event planners will tell them that they live extremely stress-filled lives because of the issues they have to face in their professional lives. That's why it's crucial for you to acquire an array of abilities in order to be successful in the industry. A majority of stressors are the result of the event planner's lack of experience or lack of experience. If you are determined to develop your skills, you'll be able to lessen the stress you face in your work. Here is a list of the abilities are essential to master during the course of your career.

Organization Skills

A major, though perhaps the most essential skills that event planners must have and learn as time passes is organizational. When you're planning an event, you have the possibility for a lot of chaos to come into your life. You will need to fill many roles and have multiple responsibilities at any given moment. It is necessary to keep track of a variety of events, dates, people, items suppliers, as well as other information to ensure that a single event runs smoothly. These problems only get more complicated when you're dealing with many events at one time. In order to effectively handle all the moving parts it is essential to possess excellent organizational skills. If you don't develop your organization abilities could lead to you not being aware of the different aspects of an event that you are paying attention to at all times. In the end, by having strong organizing skills, you're doing yourself good by making sure that you avoid making the same errors you could make in your professional role. Furthermore, information that must be included to ensure success of your event are easier to access when you can arrange information and data in a logical manner.

Communication Skills

If you're planning an event you will be in contact with numerous people. When you begin the planning process you'll need to communicate with your client. The ability to communicate is crucial throughout this process to ensure you can truly know the requirements of your customer and also ensure that they know what you can provide them with. Communication is essential when working in a team. If you're planning large-scale events, it will benefit if you had an experienced group of people working with you. To remain organized and in sync with the way you collaborate, effective communication is crucial. Communication is crucial when you're working with other suppliers or contractors in order to make sure that you have a successful the event. Keep in mind that communication doesn't only revolve around your ability to communicate yourself in a clear and effective manner. Communication is a two-way process and it's never a an unidirectional affair. It's also about being able to listen others and be able to understand their thoughts and points of view.

Creativity

Creativity isn't only a talent that's essential in the field of arts. Naturally the moment you imagine people who are creative it's common to imagine poets, musicians, painters writers, graphic artists, writers director, and other professionals working in the creative sector. But event planners need to develop their own creativity for them to be able to attain success in their industry. When you're an event organizer it is normal to be charged with designing and constructing an whole event entirely from the ground up. It's true that a customer might approach you with a specific vision or concepts of events they'd like you to plan. It is your job as an experienced event planner to be imaginative, not only with the concept of the event, but also in the methods you use to execute it. There are times when you'll encounter certain obstacles and setbacks that need inventive solutions you to get over these obstacles. This is why it's crucial to acquire skills in creativity as an event organizer even when it's not part of the "creative" business.

Multitasking Skills

However organized the event organizer it will be almost impossible to stay out of situations that require you to be multi-tasking. In ideal circumstances, you'd like to be able to perform your job in a way with a more linear that requires you to concentrate on one thing at the same time. Unfortunately, this is not something that professionals who work in the industry of event planning will have. The process of planning events isn't always a linear one. Most of the time you'll have to handle several tasks simultaneously. Naturally, this could be very challenging for those who aren't equipped to multitask and manage several tasks at the same time. If you find yourself overwhelmed by the need to do several tasks at the same time this could pose as a hindrance working in this field. This will be a challenge when you have to manage several clients who have events that overlap.

Networking Skills

If you are starting your own event planning company, you must realize that you won't be able to handle everything by yourself. You might be highly skilled in terms of organization and creative thinking. If you don't have appropriate relationships with contractors, suppliers, and other players within the field and other stakeholders, you're not going to realize your potential to the fullest extent. When it comes to planning events networking is essential because of three main reasons. One reason is that through an effective and efficient networking strategy you will be able to expand your business and find potential talent to expand your team. Additionally, if you network effectively, you'll be able to develop genuine relationships with potential contractors and suppliers who could help you bring your dream events to reality. In addition networking is an excellent method to get your name on the market and to put your business in the spotlight of potential customers or income sources. It's especially crucial for newly-established companies that plan events to build an impressive client base via the power of word of mouth.

Versatility and Adaptability

When you speak of adaptability, it's about the ability of an individual to be able to adjust to various situations or conditions. When you talk about flexibility, you're talking about the ability of a person to acquire or master various abilities and fields of study. In a sense both of these skills are interconnected and both are vital for the success of an experienced event planner. This is particularly important if you're working towards the goal of expanding your business in event planning into one that can handle various types of occasions. If you're flexible and flexible, it's going to be much simpler to be able to handle unusual requests from customers. In essence, you'll be better placed to offer the best services opposed to someone who is rigid and cannot meet the diverse requirements of various clients. You'll also are more likely to break outside of your field or specialization area in the field of event planning if have more flexibility and are more flexible.

Persistence

Persistence isn't something that's only available to those who work in the industry of event planning however it is something that deserves to be emphasized. Like any other field of business it is essential to practice perseverance. It is important to realize that success doesn't come easy. can be achieved easily. In fact, you may need to wait for a long time before you can get the first experience of success. It's not made to be guaranteed as a person, and you're never guaranteed of anything in the business. You'll encounter plenty of rejections and setbacks. In fact, you may not be able to plan some events, or you may upset a customer every now and then. That's okay. It's an integral part of what we do. It's not easy to achieve anything worthwhile. That's why you should always remain determined. If you feel that your world makes it ever harder for you to be successful The more you must fight.

Attention to Detail

As an event organizer, there are many aspects that you have to keep on top of to ensure that your event runs smoothly. That's why it's vital that you have a keen eye for detail. In all likelihood, it's important that you have an vision of the bigger perspective and comprehend the larger picture when organizing an event. But, it's crucial to make sure that the smallest elements are properly arranged and properly put together. It's the sum of these little details that determines the success of any event. As an event organizer, you'll be the one who can observe things that your clients or guests typically overlook in the course of the course of an event. It is your responsibility to make sure that no stone goes without a scratch when it comes to the planning, design the coordination and execution of the event.

Social Skills

Another crucial skill which shouldn't be limited to the industry of event planning. It's a life-skill that is beneficial to everyone regardless of the field in which they work. If you're an event planner, you're likely to be working with many different types of people. You'll be working with members of your team as well as your contractors or suppliers or clients, as well as perhaps even people who attend the events you plan. In this regard, it is crucial to develop interpersonal skills that enable you to communicate with them in a mature and healthy way. If you also have strong social abilities, it'll be easier to connect with your friends and family members to assist you in reaching your goals.

Foresight and Contingency Planning

No matter how adept you are at organizing and managing the events. There will come a time where emergencies or disasters strike suddenly and you'll need to find a fast solution or fix. For instance, a caterer could cancel on you within a few days of the event. Or, a natural disaster such as the ravages of a hurricane or heavy rain can damage the space for your event and force you to search for a replacement one at very short notice. It could be that a bridesmaid, or groomsman is not there at the time of the wedding, and you must change them as quickly as possible. No matter what the situation, such scenarios can occur. The best event planners are those who can react fast and have plans of contingency for such situations. Event planners are also excellent at handling crises. They shouldn't be in a state of panic or panicking when there is an unplanned event. As an event organizer it is your responsibility to be in control of any circumstances you're in.

Time Management

When it comes to meetings timing is important. If you are planning an appointment with a prospective client, it is important to ensure that you arrive at the right time to impress them. It's also a good way to conduct yourself. If you decide to set an appointment date with your client or contractors, you must ensure that the deadlines are adhered to. If you establish timelines for your staff or yourself for event planning and coordination, you need to ensure that these deadlines are met. If you are prone to waste time or delay your work in the business it's going to be a challenge to keep track of all the things you have to accomplish. In the event planning process it is a constant race against time, and you need to ensure that you always come out with a win.

Financial Management Skills

As an entrepreneur, you need to be adept when it comes to money. You will never be successful in the business world when you're not responsible with the management and handling of your money. That's why it is important to learn how to manage your finances capabilities. With a better understanding and appreciation of your money, you'll be able to gain an understanding into the flow of cash in your company. This means you'll be better positioned to determine the price you will charge as an expert in your field. Furthermore, you'll be more efficient in managing the amount of money coming into and leaving your company. No matter how skilled you are at being an event organizer when you're not able to manage your money. It's impossible to maintain your event planning business by relying on planning and management skills by themselves. Also, you must familiarize your self with financial aspects of running a business.

Technological Savvy

If you're not taking advantage of technology in the present, then you're already way behind. The entire world is operated by technology nowadays. If you don't acknowledge this, then you'll end up making your business's death apex. In any field it is essential for any business owner to keep up to date with trends in technology advancement. If there are a variety of tools like software for planning events or communications tools that will help you improve your business processes, then you need to take advantage of these tools. You should make every effort to help your company become more efficient and efficient in the provision the services it offers. Most times that means using all the tools and technologies readily available to you.

Leadership

Finally, you are going to be looking to enhance your leadership abilities. Anyone who runs a business must be able to lead and managing a group of people who all have one objective. If you're starting out as the sole owner of your company and you're a solo business, then maybe your leadership skills aren't required to come to the forefront just yet. As you expand your business and add new members to your team, you're certain to need to master managing the various personalities, and ensure that you are maximizing their capabilities in helping you to achieve your goals in your professional career. The top entrepreneurs and business owners will always have the highest effectiveness as leaders since they are able to get the most value from their teams.

Practicing Good Habits

It's certainly not only about the specific capabilities you have as an event organizer. Much of it involves the practices you're implementing regularly. Keep in mind that your character is ultimately determined by the behaviors you follow consistently. Therefore, if you've got bad habits, you're probably not creating a strong persona as an event organizer. In the end, it's crucial to practice the right habits every day to end up developing a solid system for you and your business. The system will help you provide better service to the people that you provide.

Get Started on Projects Early

This is in connection with the growth skills in time management as well as organizing capabilities. If you are able to close the deal with a potential client it is crucial to begin the process whenever you could. Be aware that procrastination is going to be a problem in the planning of events. Don't wait for too long to begin on a project as most of the work involved in planning an event is usually done starting at the beginning. Additionally, it's in the initial planning and design stages when you can really lay the groundwork for the other events planning and coordination. It's not possible to make any contribution to the process of planning an event unless you are able to pass the initial stages. The majority times starting is the most difficult and slow part of planning an event. When you have laid the foundation the event will go much more easily.

Stay On Top of Metrics

It doesn't matter whether you're planning corporate or social gatherings You'll always need to be aware of your metrics. However, the quality of these metrics may differ dramatically based on the type of event you're planning. However, it is essential to pay attention to these measurements to allow you to get an accurate and precise analysis of the way your event planning is progressing. As an example, perhaps you have a client from a business that wants you to plan an event. One of the metrics your client has asked you to deal with is the collection of more than $200,000 in sponsorships. While you're organizing the event this is a measure that you must consider seriously since the success of your event for the client is contingent upon the amount of money you're in a position to raise. Another instance would be when you're planning an event that is social, such as an event for weddings, and the customer is asking you to send the appropriate number of invitations to guests who are important. This is a measurement you need to keep track of in order to be sure that the client is satisfied with the performance you've delivered as an event organizer.

Write Down and Document EVERYTHING

It doesn't matter if believe that you are the most powerful and strongest brain on the planet. Even if you think you possess photographic memory it's important to write down and record every single thing. You can take the conventional way by using notebooks and a pen. It is also possible to embrace your tech-savvy side using your tablet or cell phone. It's essential to keep track of every element that is involved in the coordination and management for an occasion. Note down the details that your client will tell you during the meeting or when you're discussing an event in the beginning.

Note down all important dates and deadlines you have set for your staff and yourself. Keep track of the contact details of all contractors and suppliers that you've collaborated with in the past. It is essential to keep a record of all the details should you really want to be successful in this field. Your brain can only manage and store a certain amount of information. Never think in writing down things.

Continuously learn more about the industry

It is the ongoing process of uncovering the extent of your ignorance. While you grow adept and skilled in the field, you need to recognize that there's still a lot to be learned about the business of event planning. First of all, it's an ever-changing business. New technology is emerging and social revolutions occurring every day. These innovations are impacting how people plan or attend and enjoy their social events. This is the reason why learning must be an ongoing process for you. Self-education is something should be a regular practice throughout your professional career. If you're only beginning your career in your career, it could be beneficial to locate a mentor someone who can provide direction and guidance to ensure you are on the right the right path for your career. Your mentor should be someone with experience and who already has gained plenty of experience and wisdom them. If you are unable to locate someone to mentor you, don't be concerned. There are many literary sources (both traditional and digital) which are available to you to use. It's just the matter of spending the time to seek for these sources of information to ensure that you are able to keep a steady flow of pertinent information and data flowing your way. Also, keeping up-to-date on the latest trends in your field is going give you an edge over your competitors.

Research Existing Technologies

Don't be a snob to technology. If you're not able to make technology your partner and not your enemy, you're unlikely to make it very far in this industry. This is an aspect that is repeated frequently throughout the book. This is the reason it's vital to incorporate this practice into your everyday routine. Don't be afraid of examining the brains and strategies of your competition in this industry. Discover how they're operating their business and what tools they're employing. There are a variety of technological tools and software on the market that you can incorporate into your company as well. However, in the beginning, implementation of technology can be intimidating and costly. In the end, however, over time technological advancement could be the most efficient way to manage certain areas in your company. Explore the different technologies out there, which you can utilize for managing your operations, scheduling accounting, communication events, event design, the like. If this technology will aid you as a company manager provide better service to your potential customers They are certainly worth the investment. All it boils down to your ability to take advantage of the various tools readily available to you. If you are able to gain an advantage in the market through the an use of technologies, you ought to seriously think about making use of technology.

Embrace Social Media

Nowadays, the integration of social media in all aspects of the commercial world is expected. If you're not using social media, you're obscuring yourself to a huge number of people. In the business world the importance of visibility is paramount. You won't succeed in securing projects if your target market isn't aware of your existence. Social media has a lot to do for you when it comes to advertisement and marketing. Apart from that social media can be an extremely effective communication tool. Its nature of communication is both external and internal also. It is possible to use social media platforms to interact with the other members of your team. However, you can also utilize it to interact with customers as well as sponsors, suppliers guests, suppliers, and any other person who is involved in an event. Social media has proven to be much more than an ephemeral trend. It's certainly going to be around for the long haul. Therefore, as an entrepreneur responsible you must be prepared to learn the technique that is using the social web in the planning of events.

Expand Your Network and Nurture Relationships

One of the most damaging actions you can take as an owner of a business in the field of event planning is to be a slave to. There is always going be value in having the ability to broaden your reach and connect with different kinds of individuals and organizations. It is impossible to predict whether a potential contractor or supplier will be useful for the particular event you're managing. You don't know when your client will recommend you to a potential customer. You don't know if the person you choose to hire might be the person who can assist in taking your business to the next stage. It's great you're self-confident and trust that you can accomplish things by yourself. But, there's going to be much more value in the ability to establish a good relationship with the people you collaborate with. The most effective business owners are those who are able to connect with others who will add value to their business ventures. It's certainly not about making friends with any person. It's about being strategically making sure that those who can aid you are readily reachable and are willing to help you achieve your pursuit of your goals.

Gather Feedback Consistently

It is also crucial to ensure that you collect feedback on a regular basis. This is a suggestion that could be applied to every aspect of the way you manage your business. From your employees, collect regular feedback about how you're an executive and how you run the operations of your company. From your clients, constantly get feedback on the way you offer your services and the possible areas of improvement you can make moving forward. When you host events, collect feedback from your guests suppliers, contractors, and guests to get their feedback on their experience having worked with your company. The truth is it's possible that not all feedback will be positive and you're not always happy with the feedback you receive. However, it's by collecting feedback that you can gain an insight into your business previously unobtainable to you. It's always nice to know that you are able to look at things from the perspective of others, so that you're not restricted to your own personal and narrow view of things. Although you may have an eye for particulars, there's an opportunity to miss the things that other people might have observed.

Final Thoughts

As you might have realized by now how to become an effective event planner isn't exactly the most straightforward one found in the cookbook. As with other recipe that is complex there are many elements that require your attention, and you're given the obligation of managing each of them. Of course, nobody would expect you to handle things flawlessly when you're just beginning your journey. It's likely to take a significant amount of time to become proficient when running your business. But with constant training and perseverance over time things will pick up and you'll start to recognize the strengths of being an entrepreneur and event organizer.

It's vital to remember that the abilities and practices mentioned in this chapter are likely assist you as an event planner, it's equally crucial to keep in mind that you don't need to stress yourself out in this area. It's very beneficial if you have all of these talents to use as an event organizer. However, you shouldn't be too smug over the lack of certain skills. Event planners of different backgrounds are likely to possess different strengths, however, they'll also have weaknesses too.

It's your mission to make the most of your strengths while working on your weak points. So, you're always striving to become the best event planner you can be.

PROMOTING YOUR EVENT PLANNING BUSINESS

I

It's not enough that you are a competent event planner on your own and you've built an extremely solid event planning company with a solid group of skilled individuals who work under your. Of of course, there are numerous challenges associated with managing an event planning business. It is essential to keep up-to-date with market trends, recruiting and operations management, as well as networking accounting, and many more. However, you need to pay particular focus on marketing and promotions. Perhaps you've built an elaborate event-planning machine here. But it's not likely to have an impact when people don't know about your existence.

It should be among the main objectives of any corporate identity to communicate their brand's message to a wider audience in order to raise awareness about their services and products. Nowadays, as the world fills with ever-growing numbers of people, it indicates the growth of a market. As the market expands as does the demand for certain sectors. This is particularly true for the event planning industry. As the owner of your business you must make it a point to connect with markets that are not being explored to ensure that your company is seen and readily accessible. You operate in a highly turbulent and extremely competitive market. Your company is likely to require a strategy to get an edge or gain to stay in the game.

The growth of customers is incredibly crucial when you're considering expanding your business. Of course your more accomplished you get as an business owner, the more detailed your plans and visions will be. You'll want to increase the size of your company to be able to meet rising demand. However, it will arrive at a point when the growth rate of your business will begin exceed the rate of expansion of demand. If that occurs, it means that you must begin increasing your efforts to generate demand by gaining access to new markets.

But, creating demand is more difficult to accomplish than it appears. Actually it is the part of business that a majority of entrepreneurs struggle with. They can offer top-quality services or develop top-quality products. They lack the market's demand to earn revenue or sales. Demand growth organically is very beneficial. This means you have a sound business plan in place and that customers are genuinely confident in what you are selling. In order to break through that wall, you have to sometimes experiment with inorganic methods of marketing and advertising your company. Your company can only be larger than the market it serves. If you restrict your business to a closed-off section in the marketplace, you're restricting the growth of your company.

Sometimes, it's the matter of exploring different niches in the industry. Some will opt to set up establishments or stores in new areas to gain access to an entirely new market. There are a myriad of methods one could approach marketing or promoting. It's all about you deciding what your business goals are , and then deciding on is the most efficient course of action for your business would be.

Don't be worried if you're lost in this matter. You're an event organizer. It's not the job of a branding strategist, or marketing specialist. You're not a professional in promotional. You're able to plan events however, you do not have a lot of experience advertising businesses or reaching out to markets. But that does not mean you have to abandon your efforts. While the world of promotional activities and marketing can seem daunting and abrasive but you shouldn't be intimidated.

This chapter will provide you with a greater understanding of the field of promotions as well as how you can use them to help your company expand its reach to a wider audience. It is important to realize that there's no one-size-fits-all method of marketing. Different methods will be effective for different companies and the different audiences they serve. It's your obligation as a business owner thoroughly understand the different methods of marketing, so that you can determine which one is the most suitable for your needs. It's not necessary to go between different sources in order to get the information you need. This chapter will provide a summary of the most effective methods in marketing and promotions for businesses that plan events in the current era. However, that's not to suggest that you shouldn't look at other sources, too. In all likelihood, you should exhaust all resources available to you. Also, it is very beneficial to gain insights and gain perspective into particular industries to ensure you are proficient in them all.

Expand Your Network

It's all about who you are. In every industry networking is crucial in order to boost growth for your company. If you're always trying to grow your network, you're also expanding the visibility and reach of your company's name. Although you shouldn't be too snobby about your method of network, there's specific types of people that are worth looking for in your networking. It is recommended to intensify your efforts to network with the following groups of people:

Politicians

If you provide corporate event-planning services, you must meet the local leaders in your community and political figures. Most of the time, they are the people who are consistently participating in and organizing events. Naturally it is a business that could offer you lots of opportunities for business. Additionally having a network of government contacts will assist you when it comes to getting permits and other things for certain occasions.

Entrepreneurs/Business Owners

If you're working in the corporate event planning sector, then you'll would like to meet with the most business owners and entrepreneurs regularly as you can. If they're managing start-ups as well as Fortune 500 companies, these individuals may be in need of your help. Get in touch with local entrepreneurs and business owners. Make sure they are aware about you and your company so that they will keep you in mind anytime they have to plan parties or events.

Caterers/Stylists/Musicians/Entertainers/Part y Rental Companies

You may not be aware of it but the expansion of your suppliers' network will help with the promotion of your company and also. Yes, you've got your list of caterers and stylists who can assist you whenever you require them for an event. You don't know when they could become your marketing partners too. If you develop solid working relations with your contractors, they may do the same and recommend them to their customers as well.

Event Space Managers

A great tip you can try is to get in touch to event managers, and provide assistance to the event space managers. Most times, these event space managers do not have in-house coordinators or a management team to oversee their events. This is precisely the place you can help. Make offers of partnerships to the managers of events and have them recommend your company to their customers.

Invest in Marketing and Advertising Experts

In order to make greater profits, you're likely have to invest some cash. It's a common phrase in the business world and it's still true in the present. While it might be counterintuitive to invest in something that isn't guaranteed to yield immediate benefits but you must think about investing in advertising and marketing campaigns. Naturally, the primary purpose of this chapter is to provide you with the different methods you can implement your own strategies for promotion. But, if you're feeling that you don't be able to dedicate the necessary time, or skills to manage the campaigns, there's an alternative solution. The only thing is that you're going need to pay money to accomplish this.

It's fine to consider hiring the expertise of other individuals to manage your advertising and marketing campaigns on your behalf. That's what a lot of successful and large companies regularly do. When you decide to grow your business you'll need focus your energy and attention to more tasks. This means you don't be able to afford being more focused on potential promotional campaigns you can manage yourself. This is the reason it's justifiable to seek out expert advice in the area of advertising or marketing. This can be done by one of two ways:

Create a Dedicated Marketing or Branding Department

The first thing you can do is establish an internal advertising or marketing group for the business. The way it works is that these people will work for your company as part of your team. Their sole function is to create as well as oversee and implement marketing and branding strategies for your business. So, you'll will have people that work directly under you and who can take a lot of work off your hands. But having a department like that under the payroll of a company may not be the most cost-effective option for all firms, particularly those that are just starting out. This is why we have another option...

Hire a Brand and Marketing Consultant/Agency

There is no need to hire employees from your company to handle marketing and branding campaigns. You can contract these services out to experts and companies. They will be able provide the same level of service that an internal marketing and branding team can provide, not require the payroll of your company's monthly. You could hire these companies on a retainer or contract basis, based on the requirements of your company. This might the most economical approach to hire branding specialists. The only drawback to this approach is that you won't have the same level of accessibility that an internal team in a position to offer you.

Get Business Cards Made

It's true that using the business card may appear to be a basic and outdated idea. However, don't be too as quick to dismiss the value of this small promotional tool. Yes, we are living in a digital world where everything that has to be read is displayed on screens today. But there's still an opportunity for professional printed business cards. In the world of business the need to have an official business card on hand has more significance than practical. Of course, nowadays it is possible to look someone online and discover all you have to know about the person. However, a business card is the only way to let people be aware that you have a business intention.

While you have some creative freedoms when designing your business cards however, you must ensure that your card is functional and professional. Your basic details should be provided. If not, people won't view any seriousness from your card, and they won't consider your business seriously either. You must include names, titles, company name, address for business as well as your field of expertise, specificization, logo, and important contact details (email address, phone number and Twitter handles). If you truly want to be a part of the digital age many people are incorporating QR codes into your business cards. Most often, these QR codes lead to the website of the company or social media sites when they are clicked.

Be aware that the business card can be an excellent way to kick the conversation or close it with people. If you are able to approach someone by introducing yourself and give the person your card while you create a sales pitch for your company. It is also possible to make an informal pitch for your company when you finish a conversation with the person by handing your business card in a casual manner. One of the greatest advantages of cardholders is the fact that they're small and convenient for you to keep around. It's best to keep several business cards in your bag always. You don't know who you're likely meet or when you'll need to make a short appeal to someone.

In any field it is important to have business cards. They are particularly important when your job requires you to connect with a large number of people. This is the reason why companies that plan events must make sure they have the right company cards and business card holders for all their employees.

Conduct Email Marketing

Marketing via email may seem like an annoying and annoying method of promoting your company yet there's no doubt its efficacy. If you've ever purchased something from the internet and you've done so, then you recognize how frustrating it can be to receive emails from various businesses and brands regarding promotions which they're running. Why do you want to join this movement? It is a good idea to join the movement as it's effective.

Admit it. While you could receive hundreds of emails which you send to your spam box at least once occasionally an email likely to draw your eye and get you intrigued. It could be a sales of your favorite clothing brand or an ongoing promotion of an airline you've traveled with the internet, email marketing is effective. For the hundred emails you've sent out , which are not noticed it is likely to be one that is able to attract an interest of a potential customer. The possibility of winning this potential client's attention that makes the marketing of emails worthwhile.

But, you don't have to keep on ignoring emailing several different accounts. You must be careful regarding it, too. Make an inventory of potential contractors, suppliers, vendors as well as venue providers and customers. You should be more specific when you send emails. Make sure your emails contain high-quality content. This isn't true when they claim that bad press isn't necessarily bad press. If you go overboard with your abrasiveness in marketing via email, you may get a bad reputation. In addition, as was said, a bad name in the field of event planning is bad for business.

If you can, consider personalizing the contents of your emails based on the recipients you're sending emails to. If you're trying reach corporate clients, you should create special emails that are specifically tailored to their requirements. If you're trying to reach out to customers and suppliers, develop emails that are targeted to their needs as well. The idea is that you should be specific when it comes to mass-mailing. There is a greater chances of getting people to engage through being more intimate about the message.

Get on Social Media

It's possible that this is a regular pattern in the book but it's just to prove the importance of this idea. Social media is extremely beneficial to both your business and yourself particularly in the field of marketing. But we have to realize the fact that it is not going to be an asset for everyone. Don't worry. Here are a few fundamental strategies and tips to master social media. They will assist you with your branding's promotional and marketing strategies.

www.ingramcontent.com/pod-product-compliance
Lightning Source LLC
Chambersburg PA
CBHW060224030426
42335CB00014B/1334